PRACTICAL GUIDE TO REWIRE YOUR ANXIOUS BRAIN

EFFECTIVE STRATEGIES TO INCREASE WORK-LIFE BALANCE, BUILD RESILIENCE, MANAGE ANXIETY, AND BOOST OVERALL HEALTH

EVA KEENE

CONTENTS

YOUR FREE GIFT

Having the right tools is the key when it comes to achieving success in rewiring your anxious brain. As a way of saying thank you for your purchase, I want to offer you my worksheets FREE of charge.

Inside you will discover:

- A mood tracker
- Anxiety relief checklist
- Daily resilience planner
- Daily gratitude journal
- …And much more!

To get instant access, just scan the QR code below or go to:

[https://rewireyouranxiousbrain.myflodesk.com/]

If you want to really make a change in your life for the better, make sure to scan the QR code or head to the web address to gain instant access to your bonuses.

To all my loved ones who have helped me along my journey. —EK

INTRODUCTION

I remember a time when my days felt like an endless struggle. Anxiety wrapped itself around my mind, squeezing joy and energy out of my life. Every waking moment was a battle against the invisible enemy within my head. It was during my lowest point, trapped by addiction, that I realized something had to change. I reached rock bottom, but it also began a journey toward healing and resilience.

My name is Eva Keene, and like many of you, I have faced the overwhelming tides of anxiety. In my 20s, addiction took nearly a decade of my life. However, through a comprehensive treatment program, I found techniques that not only helped me manage my anxiety but also rewired my brain. These strategies became the cornerstone of my recovery and path to a balanced, fulfilling life.

This book is a culmination of my experiences, research, and lessons. It's a practical guide designed for busy professionals trapped by their anxious minds. I aim to provide actionable strategies and exercises to manage anxiety, improve energy, enhance mood, and boost overall health.

If you're reading this, chances are you're seeking change. You might be a stressed adult, juggling work, family, and personal responsibilities, feeling like you're constantly running on empty. You are not alone, and this book is for you.

We'll start by understanding the neuroscience behind anxiety. Knowing how your brain works can be incredibly empowering. It allows you to see anxiety not as a personal failing but as a biological response that can be managed and rewired. Throughout the book, I'll provide relatable examples and case studies to illustrate how these strategies have worked for others, including myself.

The book is structured to guide you step-by-step through this transformative journey. We'll begin with the basics of brain function and how anxiety manifests. Then, we'll move on to practical strategies for rewiring your brain, including mindfulness meditation, journaling, and positive affirmations. You'll also find tips on building resilience, achieving work-life balance, and improving your overall health.

Understanding the science behind anxiety is crucial. Our brains are incredibly adaptable, thanks to neuroplasticity—the brain's ability to reorganize itself by forming new neural connections. This means that with the proper techniques, you can rewire your brain to reduce anxiety and enhance well-being. I'll break down complex neuroscience concepts into simple, digestible pieces so you can easily apply them to your daily life.

I promise you that change is possible. It won't happen overnight, and it will require effort and commitment. But with persistence, you can transform your anxious brain into a source of strength and resilience. You can regain control over your life, improve relationships, and find joy and satisfaction in your daily activities.

As you read through this book, I encourage you to take an active role in your healing journey. Try the exercises and strategies outlined in each chapter. Reflect on your experiences and be patient with yourself. Remember, this is not about perfection but progress.

I want to remind you that you're not alone in this journey. Many people, including myself, have walked this path and emerged stronger and more resilient. You have the power to change your brain and your life. Let's take this journey together, one step at a time.

Welcome to a new beginning. Welcome to the possibility of a life less burdened by anxiety and more filled with energy, balance, and joy.

Warmly,

Eva Keene

CHAPTER 1

UNDERSTANDING ANXIETY AND YOUR BRAIN

You're sitting at your desk, staring at the screen, and your heart begins to race. Your mind starts to spiral, thinking about all the tasks you haven't completed. Your palms sweat, and it feels like the walls are closing in. This isn't just stress; it's anxiety. But what's happening inside your brain during these moments? Understanding the neuroscience behind anxiety can transform how you manage it. By knowing what triggers these responses and how your brain processes anxiety, you can apply practical strategies to regain control and find calm. This chapter aims to demystify the complexity of anxiety by breaking down its neurological basis. Understanding how your brain processes anxiety can empower you to take control and implement effective strategies for managing it.

THE NEUROSCIENCE OF ANXIETY

Our brains are intricate networks of neurons and circuits, and when anxiety strikes, specific neural pathways are activated. One of the key players in this process is the hypothalamus-pituitary-adrenal (HPA) axis. This system is responsible for your body's stress response. When you perceive a threat, the hypothalamus signals to the pituitary gland, which then triggers the adrenal glands and releases stress hormones like cortisol. This cascade prepares your body for a fight-or-flight response, increasing your heart rate and alertness. While this system is beneficial in short bursts, chronic activation can lead to persistent anxiety.

Another vital interaction in your brain involves the prefrontal cortex and the amygdala. The prefrontal cortex is responsible for higher-order functions like decision-making and rational thought, while the amygdala processes emotions such as fear and anxiety. In a well-balanced brain, the prefrontal cortex helps regulate the amygdala's response to perceived threats. However, in individuals with chronic anxiety, the amygdala often overwhelms the prefrontal cortex, leading to heightened emotional responses and difficulty in rational thinking.

Neurotransmitters play a significant role in anxiety as well. Serotonin and dopamine are two chemicals that help regulate mood and emotional responses. Imbalances in these neurotransmitters can contribute to anxiety disorders. For instance, low levels of serotonin are often associated with increased anxiety and depression. Dopamine, which is related to reward and pleasure, also affects anxiety levels; an imbalance can lead to heightened feelings of fear and stress.

Chronic anxiety doesn't only affect your brain's chemistry; it also leads to structural changes over time. One of the most affected areas is the hippocampus, which is critical for memory formation and emotional regulation. Prolonged exposure to the stress hormones like cortisol can reduce the volume of the hippocampus, impairing its functions. The default mode network (DMN) is a network of brain regions that becomes active when you're at rest and not focused on the outside world, also shows altered connectivity in people with chronic anxiety. These changes can make it harder to switch off anxious thoughts and focus on the present.

Scientific studies have provided insights into the neuroscience of anxiety. Functional magnetic resonance imaging (fMRI) studies show that individuals with anxiety disorders often have increased activity in the amygdala and reduced activity in the prefrontal cortex. Longitudinal studies on people with generalized anxiety disorder (GAD) have revealed that chronic anxiety can lead to long-term changes in the brain structure and function. Research on stress hormones has shown that elevated cortisol levels can negatively impact brain plasticity, making it harder for the brain to adapt and change.

Understanding the neuroscience of anxiety has practical implications for managing it effectively. For instance, knowing that the amygdala is hyperactive can guide you to tailor mindfulness practices specifically designed to calm this part of the brain. Techniques like progressive muscle relaxation and deep breathing can help reduce amygdala activity, making it easier to manage anxiety. Cognitive behavioral techniques (CBT), which focus on changing thought patterns, can strengthen the prefrontal cortex's ability to regulate emotions. Consistent physical exercise is also crucial, as it promotes overall brain health and can help balance neurotransmitter levels.

Armed with this knowledge, you can approach anxiety management more strategically. By understanding the underlying mechanisms, you can choose effective practices tailored to your brain's unique needs. This scientific foundation will be a sturdy platform to build a more resilient, balanced, and fulfilling life.

HOW NEUROPLASTICITY CAN HELP REWIRE YOUR BRAIN

Neuroplasticity is the brain's remarkable ability to reorganize itself by forming new neural connections. This concept is particularly significant when it comes to managing anxiety. Imagine your brain as a dynamic, adaptable network that can change and rewire based on your experiences, thoughts, and actions. Neuroplasticity means that your brain is not static; it has the potential to change, adapt, and improve. For those grappling with anxiety, this ability is a beacon of hope. Engaging in specific activities and practices can encourage your brain to form new, healthier pathways that reduce stress and enhance well-being.

One powerful example of neuroplasticity in action is seen in stroke recovery. When a person suffers a stroke, parts of the brain can be damaged, leading to loss of function. However, the brain can often compensate for lost functions through rehabilitation and targeted exercises by rerouting signals through undamaged areas. This ability to adapt and find new pathways is the essence of neuroplasticity. Similarly, in the context of anxiety, we can engage in practices that promote positive neural changes, helping to diminish anxiety over time.

Mindfulness meditation is one such practice that profoundly impacts brain structure. By regularly engaging in mindfulness meditation, individuals can increase the density of gray matter in areas of the brain that are associated with emotional regulation and self-awareness. This practice helps to calm the brain's fear center and enhance the prefrontal cortex's ability to regulate emotions.

Another effective technique is learning new skills. Whether it's picking up a new language, learning to play a new musical instrument, or trying a new hobby, engaging in new and challenging activities stimulates the formation of those new neural pathways, promoting positive neuroplasticity.

Physical exercise plays a critical role in enhancing neuroplasticity. Regular physical activity increases the production of neurotrophic factors, which support the growth and survival of neurons. Exercise boosts overall brain health and helps balance neurotransmitter levels, reducing anxiety and improving mood. Running, swimming, or brisk walking can significantly impact brain structure and function, promoting a more resilient and adaptable brain.

Scientific evidence supporting neuroplasticity is robust and convincing. Research on the effects of mindfulness shows regular meditation practice can lead to more gray matter in the hippocampus and decreased density in the amygdala, the brain's fear center. These structural changes are associated with reduced anxiety and improved emotional regulation. Studies on CBT demonstrate that this approach can lead to functional changes in the brain, particularly in cognitive control and emotional regulation areas. Neuroimaging studies reveal that regular physical exercise can increase the capacity of the hippocampus and improve connectivity in brain networks related to mood regulation.

To implement neuroplasticity-promoting activities in your daily life, begin by setting aside time for mindfulness meditation. Even 10 minutes a day can make a difference. Find a quiet space, focus on your breath, and observe your thoughts without judgment. Incorporate physical exercise into your routine by choosing activities you enjoy. Make exercise a regular part of your life, whether it's a morning jog, an evening yoga session, or a weekend hike. Lastly, challenge yourself to learn something new. Take up a new hobby, enroll in a class, or explore a new interest. These activities stimulate your brain, encouraging the formation of new, healthier pathways.

Incorporating these practices into your daily routine can seem daunting initially, but start small and build gradually. Consistency is key. By making these activities a regular part of your life, you can harness the power of neuroplasticity to rewire your brain, reduce anxiety, and enhance your overall well-being. Your brain's ability to change and adapt is a powerful tool in your journey toward a calmer, more balanced life.

THE AMYGDALA AND ITS ROLE IN ANXIETY

The amygdala is a small, oval cluster of nuclei located deep within the brain's temporal lobe. Despite its size, the amygdala plays a significant role in processing emotions, especially fear and anxiety. When you encounter something you think is a threat, the amygdala springs into action, triggering the fight-or-flight response. This ancient survival mechanism prepares your body to confront or escape danger. Your heart rate spikes, muscles tense, and your senses become hyper-alert. This response has helped humans survive for millennia, but in today's world, where threats are often psychological rather than physical, an overactive amygdala can become a source of chronic anxiety.

The amygdala doesn't work in isolation. It is closely related to other brain regions, particularly the prefrontal cortex. While the amygdala quickly reacts to potential threats, the prefrontal cortex is responsible for higher-order functions like rational thinking and decision-making. Ideally, these two parts of the brain work together; the amygdala alerts you to danger, and the prefrontal cortex assesses whether the threat is real and decides how to respond. However, in individuals with anxiety disorders, the amygdala can overpower the prefrontal cortex, making it challenging to regulate emotional responses and think clearly.

Memory formation is another crucial function of the amygdala. It helps encode emotional memories, which can be both a blessing and a curse. On one hand, remembering dangerous situations enables you to avoid them in the future. On the other hand, the amygdala's involvement in memory formation means that traumatic or stressful events can leave a lasting imprint, making it easier for the brain to trigger anxiety in similar situations later on.

Hyperactivity of the amygdala is a hallmark of many anxiety disorders. This heightened state of alert makes individuals more sensitive to perceived threats, even in relatively safe environments. Everyday situations—like giving a presentation at work or attending a social gathering—can become sources of intense anxiety. This heightened sensitivity not only makes life more challenging but also makes it harder to regulate emotional responses. The amygdala's constant readiness can lead to difficulty calming down, even when the perceived threat has passed.

Calming an overactive amygdala requires strategies to help reset this part of the brain. Deep breathing exercises are a simple and powerful way to achieve this. Focusing on slow, deliberate breaths activates the parasympathetic nervous system, which counteracts the fight-or-flight response. Another technique is progressive muscle relaxation, where you systematically tense and then relax different muscle groups. This practice reduces physical tension and sends calming signals to the amygdala.

Visualization techniques are another powerful tool. Imagine a professional who suffers from public speaking anxiety. By visualizing a successful presentation calmly and in control, individuals can train their brains to associate public speaking with positive outcomes rather than fear. This technique can help desensitize the amygdala to the stressor, making it easier to manage anxiety in real-life situations.

Consider the case of a student who experiences test anxiety. Progressive muscle relaxation has proven to be a lifesaver for many in this situation. Before an exam, the student finds a quiet space, sits comfortably, and begins to tense and relax each muscle group, starting at the toes and working up to the head. This practice reduces physical tension and calms the mind, making it easier to focus on the test than the anxiety it provokes.

Understanding the amygdala's role in anxiety empowers you to take control of your emotional responses. You can calm this overactive part of your brain by implementing strategies like deep breathing, progressive muscle relaxation, and visualization. These techniques are not only theoretical; they have been used successfully by many individuals to manage their anxiety and lead more balanced lives.

UNDERSTANDING COGNITIVE DISTORTIONS

When anxiety takes hold, our thoughts often become distorted, amplifying our fears and making situations seem far worse than they are. These cognitive distortions are habitual ways of thinking that are biased and inaccurate, leading to heightened anxiety and stress. Understanding these distortions is the first step in challenging and changing them.

One common cognitive distortion is catastrophizing, where you always expect the worst-case scenario to unfold. Imagine you have a presentation at work. Instead of focusing on your preparation, you become consumed by the thought that you'll forget everything, embarrass yourself, and maybe even lose your job. This kind of thinking not only increases your anxiety but also prevents you from performing at your best.

Another distortion is black-and-white thinking, where you see situations in extremes—perfect or a total disaster, with no middle ground. This thinking can make you feel like a mistake defines your entire worth. For example, if you make an error at work, you might think, "I'm a complete failure," instead of recognizing that everyone makes mistakes and it's part of the learning process.

Overgeneralization is yet another cognitive distortion. It involves making broad conclusions based on a single event. If you have received negative feedback on a project, you might think, "I can't do anything right," even though you've had many successes in the past. This kind of thinking traps you in a cycle of negativity and prevents you from seeing the broader picture.

These cognitive distortions create a feedback loop between distorted thoughts and anxious feelings. When you think in these biased ways, your anxiety intensifies, leading to more distorted thoughts, and the cycle continues. This loop can also lead to avoidance behaviors. For instance, if you catastrophize about social situations, you might start avoiding them altogether, which reinforces your anxiety and makes it even harder to break out of these patterns.

Cognitive behavioral techniques can be incredibly effective in challenging and changing these cognitive distortions. One powerful tool is the thought record, where you track and analyze your anxious thoughts. By writing down the situation, your automatic thoughts, and the emotions they trigger, you can see patterns and question the validity of these thoughts. This exercise helps you distance yourself from your negative thinking and view it more objectively.

Evidence-based questioning is another technique that can counter distorted thinking. Ask yourself, "What evidence supports this thought?" and "Is there an alternative explanation?" This process helps you challenge the accuracy of your anxious thoughts and replace them with more balanced and realistic ones. For example, if you're worried about an upcoming meeting, ask yourself, "What evidence do I have that it will go poorly?" and "Have I successfully handled meetings before?"

Reframing techniques can also be beneficial. Instead of focusing on the negative aspects of a situation, try to find a more positive or neutral perspective. For instance, if you didn't perform as well as you hoped in a presentation, reframe your thinking to, "I did my best, and I can learn from this experience to do better next time." This shift in perspective can reduce anxiety and help you approach challenges with a more positive mindset.

To practice cognitive restructuring, you can use daily journaling prompts to identify and challenge cognitive distortions. Start by writing about a situation that triggered anxiety, then identify the thoughts and distortions involved. Next, challenge these thoughts with evidence-based questioning and reframe them to be more balanced. This practice can help you create a habit of thinking more rationally and reduce the impact of cognitive distortions on your anxiety.

Role-playing exercises can also be helpful. Practicing alternative perspectives in a safe and controlled environment can make you more comfortable with challenging distorted thoughts. This can be particularly helpful for social anxiety, where you can role-play different social scenarios and practice responding with balanced, rational thinking.

Guided worksheets are another practical tool for cognitive restructuring. They can help you systematically identify, challenge, and reframe cognitive distortions. Following a structured format can make the process more manageable and effective.

Understanding and challenging cognitive distortions is a crucial step in managing anxiety. By recognizing these biased ways of thinking and using cognitive behavioral techniques to challenge them, you can break the cycle of anxiety and develop a more balanced and positive mindset. This reduces anxiety and empowers you to face challenges with greater confidence and resilience.

CHAPTER 2
IMMEDIATE RELIEF TECHNIQUES FOR CALMING ANXIETY

One evening, after a particularly stressful day at work, I sat in my car, unable to move. My mind was racing, my heart pounding. The overwhelming feelings of anxiety had paralyzed me. That's when I remembered a simple mindfulness exercise I had learned in therapy. I closed my eyes, took a deep breath, and focused on the present moment. Within minutes, I felt a sense of calm wash over me. That experience was a turning point, showing me the power of mindfulness in managing anxiety.

FIVE-MINUTE MINDFULNESS PRACTICES

Mindfulness is rooted in the ancient traditions of meditation, yet it has found a solid place in modern psychology. At its core, mindfulness means focusing on the present moment without judgment. It includes paying attention to your thoughts, feelings, and sensations as they arise and accepting them without trying to change or judge them. This simple and powerful practice can significantly reduce stress and increase emotional regulation. When you practice mindfulness, you create a space between your thoughts and reactions, allowing you to respond to situations more calmly and thoughtfully.

Body Scan Meditation

Let's explore some guided mindfulness exercises that can be done in just five minutes. One effective technique is body scan meditation:

1. Begin by finding a quiet place where you won't be disrupted. Sit or lie comfortably, close your eyes, and take a few deep breaths.
2. Start by focusing on your toes, noticing any sensations, whether tingling, warmth, or tension.
3. Gradually move your attention up through your feet, legs, torso, arms, and finally to your head, taking time with each part.
4. As you scan each area, consciously relax any tension you find.

This practice helps you become more aware of your body and can quickly reduce physical and mental stress.

Focused Breathing

Another effective mindfulness exercise is focused breathing. This technique is simple yet profoundly calming:

1. Sit comfortably, close your eyes, and listen to your breath.
2. Notice the feeling of the air entering and leaving your nostrils. Observe your chest and abdomen rise and fall with each breath.

3. If your mind wanders, gently bring it back to your breath
   without judgment.

A few minutes of focused breathing can help you center your mind
and reduce anxiety.

Mindful Eating

Mindfulness isn't limited to formal meditation sessions; it can be seamlessly integrated into everyday activities. Mindful eating is one such practice:

1. Instead of rushing through meals, take the time to taste each
   bite.
2. Pay attention to the textures, colors, and flavors of your food.
3. Notice the feelings in your mouth as you chew and swallow.

This practice enhances your eating experience, helps you stay present, and reduces stress.

Mindful Walking

Mindful walking is a great way to incorporate mindfulness into your daily routine:

1. Instead of letting your mind meander as you walk, focus on
   the sensations of walking.
2. Feel the ground underneath your feet with each step. Notice
   the movement of your legs and the rhythm of your breath.
3. Observe your surroundings—the sights, sounds, and smells.

This simple practice can turn an ordinary walk into a calming and grounding experience.

To make mindfulness a regular part of your routine, set reminders on your phone to take mindful breaks throughout the day. These reminders can prompt you to pause, take a few deep breaths, and return your attention to the present moment. Using mindfulness apps can also be helpful. Apps like Headspace and Calm offer guided sessions that can fit into your busy schedule, providing structure and support as you begin your mindfulness practice.

Reflection Exercise: Mindfulness Journal

Take a few moments each day to journal about your mindfulness practice. Write down what exercises you tried, how you felt before and after, and any observations or insights you gained. This can help you track your progress and deepen your mindfulness practice.

Incorporating these simple mindfulness practices into daily life can immediately relieve anxiety. By focusing on the present moment and accepting it without judgment, you can reduce stress, enhance emotional regulation, and create a sense of calm amidst the chaos of daily life.

BREATHING EXERCISES FOR INSTANT CALM

When anxiety hits, one of the quickest ways to regain control is through breathing exercises. The science behind this is both fascinating and empowering. Your breath has a direct line to your nervous system. By controlling your breath, you can activate the parasympathetic nervous system. This system is responsible for the body's rest and digestion functions. This system calms you down by slowing your heart rate and reduces the production of stress hormones like cortisol. When you breathe slowly and deeply, you signal to your brain that it's okay to relax. This can be incredibly effective in reducing anxiety almost instantly.

Deep Belly Breathing

Let's start with deep belly breathing, also known as diaphragmatic breathing. This technique is simple but powerful:

1. Sit or lie comfortably; place one hand on your chest and the other on your abdomen.
2. Breathe deeply through your nose, raising your abdomen while keeping your chest relatively still. This ensures you use

your diaphragm rather than shallowly breathing with your chest.
3. Then, exhale slowly through your mouth, feeling your abdomen fall.
4. Repeat this cycle for 5–10 breaths.

This method helps oxygenate your blood and shifts your focus away from anxious thoughts, providing immediate relief.

4-7-8 Breathing

Another effective technique is the 4-7-8 breathing exercise. This method is beneficial for calming the mind before stressful events:

1. Begin by sitting comfortably and closing your eyes.
2. Inhale quietly through your nose for a count of four.
3. Hold your breath and count to seven.
4. Then, exhale completely through your mouth, making a whoosh sound for a count of eight. This extended exhalation helps to expel more carbon dioxide from your lungs, which can have a calming effect.
5. Repeat this cycle for four breaths, gradually increasing as you become more comfortable with the technique.

Square Breathing

Square breathing, also known as box breathing, is another excellent method for reducing anxiety:

1. Sit comfortably and close your eyes.
2. Inhale through your nose for a count to four.
3. Hold your breath for a count of four.
4. Exhale through your mouth for a count of four.
5. Finally, pause and hold your breath for a count of four before starting the next round.

This technique is beneficial for grounding yourself in the present moment and can be easily practiced in various settings, whether at home, at work, or even during a commute.

These breathing exercises can be beneficial in specific situations where anxiety tends to spike. For instance, before a big presentation at work, you might find your heart racing and your palms sweating. Taking a few minutes to practice the 4-7-8 breathing technique can help calm your nerves, allowing you to focus and perform better. Similarly, during a stressful commute, deep belly breathing can transform a tense car ride into a more peaceful experience. By focusing on your breath, you can detach from the chaos around you and find a moment of calm amidst the noise.

Mastering these breathing techniques requires practice and patience. Start by practicing in a quiet, comfortable environment where you can focus simply on your breath. This will help you become familiar with the techniques and understand how they affect your body and mind. Using guided breathing apps can also be beneficial, especially when starting. Apps like Breathe2Relax and Calm offer guided sessions to help you master these exercises and integrate them into your daily routine.

Incorporating these breathing exercises into your life can provide a reliable toolkit for managing anxiety. When practiced regularly, they can become second nature, allowing you to feel calm whenever needed. Whether facing a challenging work situation, navigating a busy day, or simply looking for peace, these techniques offer immediate relief and long-term benefits.

GROUNDING TECHNIQUES TO REFOCUS YOUR MIND

Grounding techniques are practical methods designed to bring your focus back to the present moment, reduce the intensity of anxious thoughts, and help you regain control. When anxiety strikes, your mind can spiral into a whirlwind of worries, making it difficult to concentrate or feel calm. Grounding techniques act as an anchor, pulling you back to the here and now. They engage your senses and redirect your thoughts to physical sensations or external objects, providing a break from the mental chaos.

5-4-3-2-1 Technique

One of the most effective grounding exercises is the 5-4-3-2-1 technique. This method is simple yet powerful in its ability to refocus your mind:

1. To start, take a deep breath and look around you.
2. Identify five things you can see: a clock on the wall, a plant, or a book.

3. Next, focus on four things you can touch, like the texture of your clothing, the surface of your desk, or the feeling of your feet on the floor.

4. Then, listen for three sounds: the air conditioner's hum, birds' chirping, or distant traffic.

5. After that, find two smells: the scent of your coffee or a nearby candle.

6. Finally, pay attention to one taste, such as a sip of water or gum.

This exercise systematically engages your senses, pulling your attention away from anxious thoughts and grounding you in the present moment.

Physical Senses

Another grounding technique focuses on physical sensations, which can be particularly effective during acute anxiety. One method is to hold an ice cube in your hand. The intense cold immediately draws your focus, providing a sensory jolt that can break the cycle of anxious thoughts. Alternatively, you can run your hands under cold water or press your feet firmly into the ground. These physical sensations help anchor you to the present, reducing the intensity of your anxiety.

Grounding techniques are versatile and can be used in various anxiety-inducing scenarios. For instance, during a panic attack, the 5-4-3-2-1 technique can help you regain control by shifting your focus from overwhelming thoughts to tangible objects around you. Similarly, when feeling overwhelmed at work, taking a moment to focus on physical sensations, like the texture of your chair or the feeling of your pen in your hand, can provide a brief respite and help you reset.

To enhance the effectiveness of grounding techniques, practice them regularly, even when you're not feeling anxious. This helps you become more familiar with the methods and makes it easier to employ them during moments of high anxiety. Combining grounding techniques with deep breathing can also amplify their calming effects. As you practice grounding, take slow, deliberate breaths to further activate your body's relaxation response.

Create a checklist of grounding techniques that you can keep handy. Include the 5-4-3-2-1 technique, holding an ice cube, running your hands under cold water, and pressing your feet into the ground. Check off each technique as you practice it, noting how it made you feel and which were most effective.

Grounding techniques offer immediate relief from anxiety by returning your focus to the present moment. Engaging your senses and redirecting your thoughts to physical sensations or external objects can help you regain control and reduce the intensity of anxious thoughts. Whether you're experiencing a panic attack, feeling overwhelmed at work, or simply looking for a moment of calm, grounding techniques provide practical tools to help you navigate and manage anxiety.

QUICK COGNITIVE REFRAMING TASKS

Cognitive reframing is a powerful tool for managing anxiety. It involves changing how you perceive and think about a situation, reducing the emotional impact of negative thoughts. This technique is effective because it shifts your focus from automatic, often irrational, thoughts to more balanced and realistic ones. When you're caught in the grip of anxiety, your mind can become a breeding ground for worst-case scenarios and catastrophic thinking. Cognitive reframing helps you break free from this cycle by challenging and replacing these pessimistic thoughts with more constructive perspectives.

The first step in cognitive reframing is identifying and challenging your negative thoughts. This can be done by keeping a thought record, simply a journal where you note down your anxious thoughts as they arise. For instance, if you're anxious about an upcoming meeting, write down the specific thoughts causing your anxiety. These include fears of being judged, making mistakes, or not being prepared. Once you've identified these thoughts, the next step is to challenge them. Ask yourself, "What evidence do I have that supports this thought?" and "Is there an alternative explanation?" By critically examining your thoughts, you can begin to see them for what they are—often irrational and unfounded fears.

After challenging your negative thoughts, the next step is to replace them with more balanced and realistic ones. For example, if you're worried about making mistakes in your presentation, reframe this thought to, "I've prepared thoroughly, and it's okay to make small mistakes. Everyone makes them." This shift in perspective not only reduces anxiety but also boosts your confidence. Using a thought record to document this process can be incredibly helpful. You create a tangible record of your progress by writing down your initial thoughts, the evidence for and against them, and your new, reframed thoughts. This can be a valuable resource to refer back to during future moments of anxiety.

Let's look at some specific examples of cognitive reframing in action. Imagine you have a stressful work deadline approaching. Instead of viewing it as an impossible challenge bound to overwhelm you, reframe it as an opportunity for growth. Think of it as an opportunity to showcase your skills, learn new ones, and impress your colleagues and superiors. This positive outlook can transform your anxiety into motivation, making the task more manageable.

Another common source of anxiety is social events. If you view these gatherings as daunting situations where you might embarrass yourself, try reframing them as opportunities to connect with others. Remember that most people focus more on their own experiences than on judging you. Viewing social events as opportunities to build relationships and enjoy new experiences can significantly reduce your anxiety and make these occasions more enjoyable.

For cognitive reframing to be truly effective, it's essential to practice it regularly. Like any other skill, the more you practice, the better you identify and challenge your negative thoughts. Combining cognitive reframing with mindfulness practices can also enhance its effectiveness. When you practice mindfulness, you become more aware of your thoughts and emotions as they arise, which makes it easier to catch negative thoughts early and reframe them before they spiral out of control.

Incorporating these quick cognitive reframing tasks into your daily routine can immediately relieve anxiety. By changing how you perceive and think about situations, you can reduce the emotional impact of negative thoughts and approach challenges with a more balanced and positive mindset. Whether you're dealing with work-related stress, social anxiety, or any other form of anxiety, cognitive reframing offers a practical and effective tool for managing your mental health.

In the next chapter, we'll delve into strategies for building long-term resilience, helping you create a strong foundation for managing anxiety and improving your overall well-being.

CHAPTER 3
BUILDING LONG-TERM RESILIENCE

One morning, as I was sipping my coffee and watching the sunrise, I started reflecting on the small moments that brought joy to my life. I realized that despite the chaos and stress, there were always little things to be thankful for—like the warmth of my coffee mug or the first rays of sunlight. This simple act of noticing and appreciating these small moments shifted my perspective, making me feel more grounded and less overwhelmed. I then discovered the profound impact of gratitude journaling on mental health and resilience.

THE POWER OF GRATITUDE JOURNALING

Gratitude journaling is when you regularly write down things you're grateful for. This simple act can significantly boost your emotional well-being, enhance overall life satisfaction, and reduce stress and anxiety. When you focus on what you're grateful for, you shift your attention away from what's lacking or causing stress. This shift in focus can lead to a more positive outlook on life and help you build resilience against life's challenges.

To start a gratitude journal, choose the best format for you. Some people prefer a physical journal they can hold and write in, while others opt for digital formats using apps or online tools. Once you've chosen your format, set aside specific times each day for journaling; this could be in the morning as you start your day, during a lunch break, or in the evening before bed. Consistency is critical, so try to make it a daily habit.

Begin each journaling session with prompts to help spark gratitude. Simple questions like "What made me smile today?" or "What am I thankful for right now?" can guide your thoughts. Write down at least three things you're grateful for each day. These can be big or small, from a significant achievement at work to the kindness of a stranger or simply the comfort of a warm blanket. Writing helps solidify these positive experiences in your mind, making it easier to recall them later.

Scientific evidence supports the benefits of gratitude journaling. Research has shown that gratitude practices can reduce cortisol levels, the body's primary stress hormone. Lower cortisol levels are associated with reduced stress and anxiety. Studies have also found that individuals who regularly practice gratitude have improved mood and resilience. This means they are better equipped to handle stress and bounce back from challenges more effectively.

Consider using reminders or gratitude apps to maintain a consistent gratitude journaling habit. Apps like Gratitude Journal or Grateful can send you daily prompts and reminders to help you stay on track. Sharing your gratitude entries with a friend or family member can also provide additional motivation and accountability. Discussing what you're grateful for can strengthen your social connections and enhance the positive effects of the practice.

Interactive Element: Gratitude Journal Prompts

To help you get started, here are some prompts you can use in your gratitude journal:

- What is one thing that made you smile today?
- What is something you accomplished today that you feel proud of?
- Who is someone you are grateful for, and why?
- What is a simple pleasure that you enjoyed today?
- What is something you are looking forward to?

Incorporate these prompts into your daily journaling practice to help you focus on the positive aspects of your life. Over time, you'll likely find that this practice reduces your anxiety and enhances your overall well-being and satisfaction with life. By consistently focusing on gratitude, you build a reservoir of positive experiences to help you navigate stressful times with greater ease and resilience.

HABIT-FORMING STRATEGIES FOR MENTAL HEALTH

Understanding how habits are formed can be a game-changer for your mental health. Habits are routines that our brains automate to save effort. The psychology of habit formation boils down to a simple three-step process known as the habit loop:

- cue
- routine
- reward

The cue is a trigger that initiates the behavior, the routine is the behavior itself, and the reward is the benefit you get from completing the behavior. This loop is fundamental because it explains why habits stick and how they can be changed. Repetition and consistency are crucial. The more you repeat a behavior in response to a cue, the more automatic it becomes, embedding itself into your daily routine.

The next step is identifying essential habits that positively impact your mental health. Daily mindfulness practice is one such habit. Even a few minutes of mindfulness daily can help you manage stress and anxiety more effectively. Regular physical exercise is another critical habit. Exercise releases endorphins, which are natural mood lifters. It also helps regulate sleep patterns and reduces stress. Consistent sleep schedules are equally important. Going to bed and waking up at the same time every day helps stabilize your internal clock, improving the quality and duration of your sleep. These habits build a strong foundation for mental resilience.

Building new habits can seem daunting, but starting small makes it manageable. Focus on one habit at a time. Changing too many behaviors at once can lead to overwhelm and burnout. Once you've chosen the habit you want to build, use habit stacking to link it to an existing habit. For example, if you start meditating daily, do it right after brushing your teeth in the morning. This creates a natural cue for your new habit. Tracking your progress can also be incredibly motivating. Use a habit tracker or app to monitor your progress and celebrate small wins.

Challenges are inevitable when forming new habits. Setbacks happen, but they don't mean failure. The key is maintaining motivation and getting back on track as soon as possible. Finding accountability partners can be a significant help. Share your goals with a friend or family member who can offer support and encouragement. Adjusting habits to fit changing schedules is also crucial. Life is unpredictable, and flexibility can make sticking with your new habits easier. If your routine changes, find a new time or way to incorporate your habit into your day.

Reflection Exercise: Habit-Tracking Template

Create a simple habit-tracking template to help you monitor your progress. List the habits you're working on and daily checkboxes to mark each day you complete the habit. Review your progress at the end of the week and reflect on what worked well and what could be improved. This practice keeps you accountable and helps you identify patterns and make necessary adjustments.

Understanding the psychology behind habit formation can significantly impact your mental health journey. You can build a more resilient and balanced life by focusing on critical habits, starting small, and overcoming obstacles with practical strategies.

BUILDING A DAILY MEDITATION PRACTICE

Meditation can be a game-changer for managing anxiety and building resilience. Incorporating meditation into your daily life creates a powerful tool for reducing stress and anxiety. Meditation helps calm the mind, making it easier to focus and concentrate on the tasks. It also enhances emotional regulation, allowing you to respond to life's challenges with ease and poise. These benefits can transform your mental landscape, providing a sense of inner peace and balance that supports long-term resilience.

There are various types of meditation practices you can explore, each offering unique benefits. Mindfulness meditation involves paying attention to the present moment without judgment. This practice helps you become more aware of your thoughts and feelings, reducing their overwhelming power. On the other hand, loving-kindness meditation focuses on cultivating compassion and kindness toward yourself and others. This practice can help reduce negative emotions and foster a sense of connectedness. Body scan meditation involves systematically focusing on different parts of your body, noticing sensations, and releasing tension. This practice can be particularly effective for relieving physical stress and promoting relaxation.

Starting a daily meditation practice might seem daunting, but it doesn't have to be complicated. Begin by choosing a time and place for meditation that fits seamlessly into your daily routine. It could be first thing in the morning, during a lunch break, or before bed. The key is to be consistent. Start with short sessions of just 5–10 minutes. As you become more comfortable, gradually increase the duration of your meditation sessions. Guided meditation apps or recordings can provide structure and support, especially if you're new to meditation. Apps like Headspace, Calm, and Insight Timer offer a variety of guided sessions that cater to different needs and preferences.

Common challenges often arise when you start meditating, but keep them from deterring you. Restlessness and distraction are typical, especially in the beginning. Instead of getting frustrated, acknowledge these feelings and gently bring your focus back to your breath or the meditation prompt. Over time, your ability to stay present will improve. Finding the motivation to meditate regularly can also be challenging. To stay motivated, remind yourself of the benefits you've experienced and the progress you've made. Combining meditation with other relaxation techniques, such as deep breathing or progressive muscle relaxation, can enhance its effectiveness and make it easier to maintain a consistent practice.

Interactive Element: Meditation Progress Tracker

Create a simple progress tracker to monitor your meditation practice. Each day, note the duration of your meditation session and any observations or insights you gained. Reflect on how you felt before and after meditating. This tracker can help you stay accountable and provide a visual reminder of your commitment to building resilience through meditation.

Incorporating meditation into your daily routine can profoundly benefit your mental health. By reducing stress and anxiety, improving focus and concentration, and enhancing emotional regulation, meditation helps you build a strong foundation for long-term resilience. Explore meditation practices to find what resonates with you, and use practical strategies to overcome common challenges. With consistency and dedication, meditation can become a powerful ally in your journey toward a more balanced and fulfilling life.

TECHNIQUES TO IMPROVE SLEEP HYGIENE

Sleep hygiene refers to the practices and habits necessary for good nighttime sleep quality and full daytime alertness. It's a cornerstone of mental health and anxiety management. Poor sleep can wreak havoc on your emotional regulation and resilience. When you're sleep-deprived, you're more likely to feel irritable, stressed, and overwhelmed. Chronic sleep deprivation can exacerbate anxiety levels, making it even harder to cope with daily challenges. On the other hand, quality sleep helps to stabilize your mood, improve cognitive function, and enhance your ability to handle stress.

Creating a sleep-friendly environment is crucial for improving sleep hygiene:

- Start by keeping your bedroom cool, dark, and quiet. A cool temperature helps your body to relax and fall asleep faster. Darkness signals your brain that it's time to wind down, so consider using blackout curtains or an eye mask. Silence can be achieved with earplugs or a white noise machine in a noisy area.
- Investing in a comfortable mattress and pillows can also make a big difference. Your bed should be a sanctuary of comfort, supporting your body and allowing you to sleep soundly through the night.
- Another essential step is reducing screen time before bed. The blue light emitted by phones, tablets, and computers can interfere with the production of melatonin, the hormone responsible for sleep. Try to shut off all screens at least an hour before bedtime and engage in relaxing activities like reading a book or taking a warm bath.
- Establishing a consistent sleep routine can significantly improve your sleep quality. Aim to go to bed and wake up simultaneously every day, even on weekends. This consistency helps regulate your body's internal clock, making it easier to fall asleep and wake up naturally.
- Developing a wind-down routine before bed can signal your body that it's time to relax and prepare for sleep. Engage in calming activities such as reading, gentle stretching, or practicing deep breathing exercises.

- Avoid caffeine and heavy meals close to bedtime, as they disrupt sleep. Instead, opt for a light snack if you're hungry, and choose herbal teas that promote relaxation.

Overcoming sleep challenges often requires practical strategies tailored to your specific needs. If you struggle with falling asleep, techniques like progressive muscle relaxation can be highly effective. This involves tensing and slowly relaxing each muscle group, starting from your toes and working your way up to your head. This practice not only reduces physical tension but also calms your mind. For those dealing with insomnia, cognitive behavioral therapy for insomnia (CBT-I) can be a game-changer. CBT-I focuses on changing the thoughts and behaviors that interfere with sleep, helping you develop healthier sleep habits. Addressing anxiety-related sleep disturbances is also crucial. Techniques such as deep breathing, mindfulness meditation, and visualization can help calm your mind and prepare your body for restful sleep.

Interactive Element: Sleep Hygiene Checklist

Create a personalized sleep hygiene checklist to help you implement these strategies. Include items such as:

- Keep the bedroom cool, dark, and quiet.
- Invest in a comfortable mattress and pillows.
- Reduce screen time an hour before bed.
- Go to bed and wake up at the same time every day.
- Develop a wind-down routine.
- Avoid caffeine and heavy meals close to bedtime.
- Practice progressive muscle relaxation.
- Consider CBT-I for insomnia.

Check off each item as you incorporate it into your routine, and adjust as needed based on your progress and feedback.

Incorporating these sleep hygiene techniques into your daily routine can significantly improve your sleep quality and overall mental health. By creating a sleep-friendly environment, establishing a consistent sleep routine, and using practical strategies to overcome sleep challenges, you'll build a strong foundation for long-term resilience. This will help you manage anxiety more effectively and enhance your overall well-being and quality of life.

As we move forward, it's essential to remember that every small step you take contributes to your overall progress. Each night of good sleep, each moment of mindfulness, and each act of gratitude builds up, creating a more resilient and balanced you. In the next chapter, we'll explore how to integrate physical health into your anxiety management strategies, providing you with more tools to support your mental well-being.

CHAPTER 4
INTEGRATING PHYSICAL HEALTH

One morning, I was staring at my reflection in the mirror, feeling utterly drained. The stress and anxiety had taken a toll on my body, and I realized I needed a significant change. I decided to lace up my old sneakers and go for a jog. The fresh air, the rhythmic pounding of my feet on the pavement, and the endorphin rush I felt afterward were transformative. That simple decision began my understanding of how physical exercise could be a powerful ally in managing anxiety.

THE ROLE OF EXERCISE IN ANXIETY MANAGEMENT

Exercise isn't only about physical health; it also profoundly impacts mental well-being. When you engage in physical activity, your body releases endorphins and serotonin, chemicals that act as natural mood lifters. These neurotransmitters help reduce stress and anxiety, promoting happiness and relaxation. The production of endorphins, often referred to as "runner's high," creates a natural euphoria, which can be incredibly effective in combating the lows associated with anxiety. Serotonin, on the other hand, helps regulate mood, appetite, and sleep, all of which can be disrupted by stress.

In addition to boosting mood-enhancing chemicals, exercise helps reduce stress hormones like cortisol. High levels of cortisol, a hormone released during stress, can exacerbate anxiety and lead to various physical health issues. Regular physical activity helps to lower cortisol levels, creating a more balanced hormonal environment that supports mental well-being. This reduction in stress hormones can make you feel calmer and more in control of your emotions.

Another significant benefit of exercise is its positive impact on sleep quality. Anxiety often disrupts sleep patterns, leading to insomnia and restless nights. Exercise promotes better sleep by helping you fall asleep faster and enjoy more profound, restorative sleep cycles. Improved sleep quality enhances cognitive function and emotional regulation, making managing anxiety during waking hours easier. When you sleep well, you wake up refreshed and better equipped to handle the day's challenges.

Regular physical activity also boosts cognitive function and focus. Exercise increases blood flow to the brain, promoting the growth of new neural connections and improving overall brain health. Enhanced cognitive function means better concentration, sharper memory, and problem-solving skills. These mental benefits can help you stay focused and productive, reducing the overwhelming feelings that often accompany anxiety.

Various types of exercise can be particularly beneficial for managing anxiety:

- Aerobic exercises like running, cycling, and swimming are excellent for releasing endorphins and improving cardiovascular health. These activities elevate your heart rate, providing a full-body workout that invigorates you.
- Strength training, such as weight lifting or resistance bands, helps build muscle and improve physical strength. This exercise can also boost self-esteem and body confidence, improving overall mental well-being.
- Flexibility exercises, including yoga and Pilates, focus on stretching and strengthening muscles while promoting relaxation and mindfulness. These practices are particularly effective in reducing physical tension and calming the mind.
- High-intensity interval Training (HIIT) combines short bursts of intense activity with periods of rest or low-intensity exercise. HIIT workouts are efficient and easily adapted to fit busy schedules, providing a quick yet effective way to manage stress and anxiety.

Creating an exercise routine that fits a busy lifestyle can seem daunting, but it doesn't have to be. Start by setting realistic goals and beginning with small, manageable steps. If you're new to exercise, aim for short sessions a few times a week and gradually increase the duration and intensity as you become more comfortable. Incorporating exercise into daily activities can also make it more accessible. Consider walking meetings, taking the stairs instead of the elevator, or doing a quick workout during your lunch break. Using technology to track your progress can provide motivation and accountability. Fitness apps and wearable devices can help you set goals, monitor your activity, and celebrate your achievements.

Consider the story of Sarah, a corporate professional who struggled with anxiety and found solace in lunchtime walks. Initially, Sarah started with short walks around her office building. As she became more comfortable, she extended her walks to nearby parks, finding that the physical activity and time spent in nature significantly reduced her anxiety. The midday break also gave her a much-needed mental reset, allowing her to return to work with renewed focus and energy.

Another inspiring example is Lisa, a new parent who combined baby and yoga sessions to manage postpartum anxiety. The gentle stretches and mindful breathing exercises helped Lisa relax and provided a bonding experience with her baby. This practice became a cherished part of her daily routine, offering physical and emotional benefits.

Interactive Element: Exercise Planning Worksheet

Create a worksheet to help you plan your exercise routine. List different types of exercises you're interested in, set realistic goals, and outline a weekly schedule. Include sections for tracking progress and reflecting on your feelings after each workout.

Incorporating regular exercise into your life can be a powerful tool for managing anxiety. Physical activity offers many mental health benefits, whether through aerobic activities, strength training, flexibility exercises, or HIIT workouts. By setting realistic goals, integrating exercise into daily routines, and using technology to track progress, you can create a sustainable exercise routine that supports your mental well-being.

NUTRITION TIPS TO BOOST MENTAL HEALTH

Understanding the gut-brain connection can be a game-changer when it comes to managing anxiety. The gut and brain communicate through a complex network known as the gut-brain axis. This connection involves the vagus nerve, hormones, and the immune system. One crucial player in this dialogue is the gut microbiome, a collection of trillions of bacteria living in your intestines. These microorganisms help regulate mood by producing neurotransmitters like serotonin and dopamine, which are crucial for emotional well-being. When your gut microbiome is healthy and balanced, it supports better mental health. However, an imbalance can lead to inflammation, which negatively affects the brain and contributes to anxiety and depression.

Inflammation is another critical factor in the gut-brain connection. Chronic inflammation can impact your mental health by disrupting the production of neurotransmitters and increasing stress hormone levels. A balanced diet is vital for maintaining gut and mental well-being.

Foods rich in antioxidants, fiber, and healthy fats can help reduce inflammation and support the production of neurotransmitters, creating a more balanced emotional state. A diet that nurtures your gut can significantly improve your mental health, making it easier to manage anxiety.

Let's explore some foods that promote mental well-being:

- Omega-3 fatty acids are essential for brain health and can be found in foods like salmon, chia seeds, and walnuts. These healthy fats support the structure of brain cells and have been shown to reduce symptoms of anxiety and depression.
- Probiotics, found in yogurt, kefir, and sauerkraut, are beneficial bacteria that help maintain a healthy gut microbiome. These foods can improve digestion and reduce inflammation, improving mental health.
- Antioxidant-rich foods like blueberries, dark chocolate, and green tea help protect your brain cells from damage caused by free radicals, which can contribute to anxiety.
- B vitamins in leafy greens, eggs, and legumes are crucial in neurotransmitter production and energy metabolism, supporting overall mental well-being.

While certain foods can boost your mental health, others can exacerbate anxiety and should be limited or avoided:

- Caffeine, found in coffee and energy drinks, can increase feelings of anxiety and disrupt sleep patterns. If you're anxious, consider reducing your caffeine intake or switching to decaffeinated options.
- Refined sugars in candies, pastries, and sugary drinks can cause blood sugar spikes and crashes, leading to mood swings and increased anxiety.
- Alcohol is another substance that can negatively impact mental health. While it may provide temporary relief, alcohol can interfere with sleep and exacerbate anxiety in the long run.

- Processed foods high in trans fats, like fast food and packaged snacks, can contribute to inflammation and negatively affect brain health, making anxiety management more challenging.

Incorporating mental health-boosting foods into your diet can be easier than you think. Start with simple meal planning and preparation ideas. Plan your meals for the week, focusing on whole, nutrient-dense foods. Preparing meals in advance can save time and reduce the temptation to reach for unhealthy options. Easy and healthy snack options include a handful of nuts, a piece of fruit, or a yogurt parfait with berries and a sprinkle of chia seeds. These snacks provide a quick nutrient boost and help maintain stable blood sugar levels.

Experiment with recipes for balanced meals that include protein, healthy fats, and fiber. For example, try a quinoa salad with leafy greens, grilled salmon, avocado, and a lemon-tahini dressing. This meal is rich in omega-3s, antioxidants, and B vitamins, supporting gut and brain health. Using a food diary to track dietary impacts on your mood can provide valuable insights. Note how you feel after eating certain foods and identify patterns that affect your mental well-being. This practice can help you make informed choices about what to include or avoid in your diet.

Interactive Element: Balanced Meal Recipe

Try this simple and nutritious recipe to boost your mental health:

Quinoa and Kale Power Bowl

Ingredients:

- 1 cup cooked quinoa
- 2 cups chopped kale
- 1/2 cup chickpeas
- 1/4 avocado
- 1 tbsp olive oil
- 1 tbsp lemon juice
- salt and pepper to taste

Instructions:

1. Toss the kale with olive oil, lemon juice, salt, and pepper.
2. Add the cooked quinoa, chickpeas, and avocado.
3. Mix well and enjoy a meal rich in antioxidants, fiber, and healthy fats.

Understanding the gut-brain connection and making mindful food choices can significantly impact your mental health. Incorporate foods that promote well-being and avoid those that exacerbate anxiety. With practical tips for healthy eating, you can create a diet that supports your gut and brain, making it easier to manage anxiety and improve overall well-being.

SLEEP HYGIENE FOR BETTER MENTAL WELL-BEING

Quality sleep is a cornerstone of mental health and managing anxiety. When you sleep well, your brain has the opportunity to regulate emotions effectively. During sleep, particularly in the rapid eye movement (REM) stage, your brain processes emotions, consolidates memories, and clears out toxins that accumulate during the day. Emotional regulation is closely tied to sleep quality. You're better equipped to handle stress and respond calmly when well-rested. On the flip side, sleep deprivation can exacerbate anxiety, making it harder to manage daily stressors. Lack of sleep can also lead to irritability, mood swings, and impaired cognitive function. This creates a vicious cycle where anxiety disrupts sleep, and poor sleep heightens anxiety. Therefore, prioritizing sleep is not just about feeling rested; it's about maintaining your mental health and emotional stability.

Reflection Exercise: Sleep Quality Journal

Keep a sleep quality journal to track your sleep patterns and identify factors that impact your rest. Each morning, note the time you went to bed, the time you woke up, and the quality of your sleep. Reflect on any activities or thoughts that may have affected your sleep. This journal can help you identify patterns and adjust to improve your sleep quality.

Focusing on sleep hygiene can create an environment and routine that promotes restful sleep. Quality sleep supports emotional regulation, reduces anxiety, and enhances overall mental well-being. With practical techniques and a consistent bedtime routine, you can improve your sleep quality and build a foundation for better mental health.

THE IMPACT OF HYDRATION ON ANXIETY

Hydration plays a pivotal role in mental health, and its impact on anxiety is often underestimated. When you're dehydrated, your brain's function can be significantly impaired. The brain is about 75% water; even mild dehydration can affect its performance. Dehydration reduces the flow of oxygen to the brain, which can result in feelings of fogginess, fatigue, and irritability. These symptoms can exacerbate anxiety, making it harder to manage daily stressors. Water is also vital for producing neurotransmitters, the chemicals that transmit signals in the brain. Adequate hydration ensures that neurotransmitters like serotonin and dopamine are produced in sufficient quantities, helping to stabilize mood and reduce anxiety.

Dehydration also impacts cognitive performance. When your brain doesn't receive enough water, it struggles to perform complex tasks and maintain focus. This can lead to decreased mental function, making concentrating and thinking harder. For those dealing with anxiety, this cognitive impairment can heighten feelings of overwhelm and stress. Staying hydrated helps maintain mental sharpness, allowing you to manage your thoughts and emotions better.

To ensure optimal mental health, it's important to stay adequately hydrated. General recommendations suggest that women drink about 2.7 liters (91 ounces) of water daily, while men should aim for about 3.7 liters (125 ounces). These recommendations can vary based on age, sex, and activity level. For instance, if you're physically active or live in a hot climate, you may need to drink more water to stay hydrated. Signs of dehydration include dry mouth, dark urine, fatigue, and dizziness. By paying attention to these signs, you can take proactive steps to maintain proper hydration.

Calculating individual hydration needs can help you tailor your water intake to your specific requirements. A simple method is to divide your body weight into pounds by two and aim to drink that number of ounces of water each day. For example, if you weigh 150 pounds, you should consume about 75 ounces of water daily. This personalized approach ensures enough water to support your mental and physical health.

Incorporating hydration into a busy lifestyle can be challenging, but there are practical tips to help you stay on track:

- Carrying a reusable water bottle with you throughout the day can be a constant reminder to drink water. Choose a bottle you enjoy using and keep it filled and within reach.
- Setting reminders on your phone or using hydration apps can also help you remember to drink water regularly. These reminders can be handy if you get caught up in work or other activities and need to remember to hydrate.
- Incorporating hydrating foods into your diet is another effective way to boost your water intake. Cucumbers, watermelon, oranges, and strawberries have high water content and can contribute to your overall hydration. These foods not only provide hydration but also offer essential vitamins and minerals that support overall health. Including various hydrating foods in your meals and snacks can make it easier to stay hydrated without feeling like you're constantly drinking water.

Consider the story of Mark, an office worker who struggled with constant fatigue and brain fog. After learning about the importance of hydration, Mark started using a hydration app to track his water intake. He set reminders to drink water throughout the day and habitually refilled his water bottle whenever he took a break. Within a few weeks, Mark noticed a significant improvement in his energy levels and cognitive function. He felt more alert, focused, and better equipped to handle the demands of his job.

Another example is Emily, an athlete who balanced her hydration needs with her physical activity. Emily realized that she needed to drink more water on days when she had intense training sessions. She started tracking her water intake and consciously drank water before, during, and after workouts. This proactive approach helped Emily maintain her performance and reduce feelings of fatigue and anxiety associated with dehydration.

Hydration is a simple yet powerful tool for managing anxiety and improving mental health. By understanding the physiological connection between hydration and brain function, you can take proactive steps to stay hydrated. Incorporate practical tips like carrying a reusable water bottle, setting reminders, and including hydrating foods in your diet to ensure you meet your hydration needs. The stories of individuals like Mark and Emily highlight the transformative impact proper hydration can have on mental well-being, motivating you to prioritize your hydration habits.

In the next chapter, we'll explore the power of mindfulness and meditation in managing anxiety, providing additional tools to support your mental health and well-being.

CHAPTER 5
MINDFULNESS AND MEDITATION

I remember sitting in a bustling café, feeling the weight of deadlines, emails, and life's endless to-do list pressing down on me. As I sipped my coffee, I noticed a man at a nearby table. Amid the chaos, he sat with his eyes softly closed, taking slow, deliberate breaths. He radiated a calm that seemed almost out of place. It struck me then—he had found peace amid the noise and rush. That was my first real encounter with mindfulness, and it opened the door to a practice that would transform my relationship with anxiety.

STARTING WITH BASIC MINDFULNESS

Mindfulness is the practice of being fully present in the moment without judgment. It involves paying attention to your thoughts, feelings, and bodily sensations as they arise and accepting them without trying to change or judge them. This simple yet profound practice can help you break free from the grip of anxiety by shifting your focus from the overwhelming future or distressing past to the present moment.

Mindful Breathing

One of the cornerstones of mindfulness is the act of focusing on your breath. This practice, often called mindful breathing, involves paying close attention to the in-and-out rhythm of your breathing.

1. Find a quiet place to sit or lie down, close your eyes, and take a few deep breaths.
2. As you breathe in, notice the sensation of the air filling your lungs.
3. As you breathe out, feel the release of tension.
4. If your mind starts to wander—and it will—gently bring your focus back to your breath.

This practice helps anchor you in the present, providing a sense of calm and stability.

Body Scan

Another essential mindfulness exercise is the body scan. This practice involves mentally scanning and relaxing each body part, from your toes to the top of your head.

1. Begin by finding a comfortable position and closing your eyes.
2. Take a deep breath and focus your attention on your toes.
3. Notice any sensations—whether it's tension, warmth, or tingling.
4. Gradually move your attention up through your feet, legs,

torso, arms, and finally to your head, taking time with each
   part.
5. As you scan each area, consciously release any tension you
   find.

This practice enhances your awareness of bodily sensations and promotes relaxation.

Mindful Listening

Mindful listening is another simple yet effective mindfulness exercise. This practice involves paying full attention to the sounds around you without judgment.

1. Find a quiet place where you can sit comfortably and close
   your eyes.
2. Take a few deep breaths to center yourself.
3. Then, focus on the sounds you hear—the air conditioner's
   hum, leaves rustling, or distant traffic.
4. Instead of labeling or judging these sounds, simply notice
   them.

This practice helps you become more present and attuned to your environment, reducing the noise of anxious thoughts.

Starting a mindfulness practice comes with its own set of challenges. One of the most common obstacles is dealing with a wandering mind. It's natural for your mind to drift to thoughts about the past or future. When this happens, gently refocus on your breath or the present moment without judgment. Practicing patience and self-compassion is crucial. Remember, mindfulness is not about achieving a perfect state of calm but about becoming more aware and accepting of your experiences as they are.

Essential mindfulness has profound benefits, especially for reducing anxiety. One of the immediate benefits is stress reduction. Focusing on the present moment frees your mind from the constant cycle of worry and stress, providing instant relief. Mindfulness also improves emotional regulation. You can respond to situations more calmly and thoughtfully when you become more aware of your thoughts and feelings without getting attached. This heightened awareness helps you identify and address anxious thoughts and triggers before they spiral out of control.

Reflection Exercise: Mindfulness Journal

Consider starting a mindfulness journal. Write about your daily mindfulness practice—what exercises you tried, how you felt before and after, and any observations or insights you gained. This reflection can help you track your progress and deepen your practice.

Incorporating essential mindfulness into your daily life can provide immediate relief from anxiety. You can anchor yourself in the present moment by focusing on your breath, bodily sensations, and the sounds around you. This practice reduces stress and improves emotional regulation and awareness of anxious thoughts. As you continue your mindfulness journey, remember to be patient and compassionate with yourself. Every moment of mindfulness is a step toward a calmer, more balanced life.

ADVANCED MEDITATION TECHNIQUES FOR ANXIETY

Advancing your meditation practice can deepen your experience and offer enhanced benefits for managing anxiety. As you become more comfortable with basic mindfulness exercises, progressing to more sophisticated techniques can provide deeper emotional and cognitive benefits. These advanced practices can help you cultivate a greater sense of compassion, visualize calming scenarios, or use mantras to focus your mind. By engaging in these techniques, you deepen your mindfulness practice and equip yourself with powerful tools to combat anxiety more effectively.

Loving-Kindness Meditation

One advanced meditation technique you can explore is loving-kindness meditation. This practice involves cultivating compassion and kindness, first toward yourself and then extending it to others:

1. Begin by finding a comfortable seated position and closing your eyes. Take a few deep breaths to center yourself.
2. Start by silently repeating phrases of kindness and goodwill toward yourself, such as "May I be happy, may I be healthy, may I be safe."
3. After a few minutes, extend these phrases to others—starting with someone you love, then to a neutral person, and finally to someone you find challenging.

This practice helps soften the heart and reduce anger and resentment, replacing them with compassion and empathy.

Visualization Meditation

Visualization meditation is another powerful technique for managing anxiety. This practice involves imagining a safe and calming place where you feel completely comfortable:

1. Find a quiet space, close your eyes, and take a few deep breaths.
2. Picture a place that brings you peace—a beach, a forest, a cozy room, or any setting that makes you feel safe.
3. Engage all your senses in this visualization. Imagine the sounds, smells, and textures of this place.
4. Spend a few minutes fully immersing yourself in this calming environment.

Visualization helps to shift your focus from anxious thoughts to a peaceful and serene setting, providing immediate relief from anxiety.

Mantra Meditation

Mantra meditation involves repeating calming words to focus the mind and reduce mental chatter:

1. Choose a word or phrase that resonates with you, such as "peace," "calm," or "I am enough."
2. Sit in a comfortable position, close your eyes, and take a few deep breaths.
3. Begin repeating your chosen mantra silently or aloud, synchronizing it with your breath.
4. If your mind wanders, bring your focus back to the mantra.

This repetitive practice helps to quiet the mind and create a sense of inner calm. Over time, the mantra becomes a mental anchor, helping you maintain focus and composure during stressful situations.

Incorporating these meditation techniques into your daily routine can be highly beneficial. Set aside longer meditation sessions to fully engage in these practices. You might begin with a 20-minute session and gradually increase the duration as you become more comfortable. Combining different meditation techniques can also enhance their effectiveness. For example, start with a few minutes of mindful breathing to center yourself, followed by a loving-kindness meditation, and conclude with a mantra meditation. This combination allows you to experience the unique benefits of each practice, creating a well-rounded meditation routine.

Consider the story of a teacher named Ashley, who used loving-kindness meditation to reduce classroom anxiety. Ashley found that starting her day with this practice helped her cultivate compassion and patience, which she then brought into her interactions with students. The practice reduced her stress and created a more positive and supportive classroom environment. Similarly, an entrepreneur named James used visualization meditation to manage business-related stress. Before important meetings or presentations, James would spend a few minutes visualizing a successful outcome, picturing himself speaking confidently and calmly. This practice helped him reduce pre-meeting anxiety and perform at his best.

These real-life examples show the transformative power of advanced meditation techniques. Incorporating loving-kindness meditation, visualization, and mantra meditation into your daily routine can deepen your mindfulness practice and enhance your ability to manage anxiety. Whether you're a teacher, an entrepreneur, or anyone seeking to reduce stress and improve emotional well-being, these advanced techniques offer powerful tools to support your mental health.

INCORPORATING MINDFULNESS INTO DAILY ACTIVITIES

Imagine starting your day with a simple breakfast, but instead of rushing through it, you take the time to savor each bite fully. This practice, known as mindful eating, involves paying close attention to your food's flavors, textures, and aromas. Sit down with your meal, take a deep breath, and focus on the experience of eating. Notice the crunch of a fresh apple, the warmth of your coffee, or the creaminess of yogurt. Doing so creates a moment of calm and presence, turning a routine activity into a form of meditation.

Another opportunity for mindfulness is during your daily commute or a casual walk. Mindful walking involves paying attention to each step and breath. Feel the ground beneath your feet, notice the rhythm of your stride, and observe your surroundings without judgment. Whether walking through a bustling city or a quiet park, this practice helps ground you in the present moment, reducing stress and anxiety. When done mindfully, a simple walk becomes a refreshing break from the mental chatter that often accompanies our daily lives.

Even cleaning can become a mindful activity. Rather than viewing it as a chore, focus on the sensory experience of cleaning. Notice the feel of the cloth in your hand, the scent of the cleaning products, and the satisfaction of a clean surface. Immersing yourself in the task can turn a mundane activity into a meditative practice. This approach makes cleaning more enjoyable and provides a break from anxious thoughts, allowing you to engage fully with the present moment.

Work and professional settings offer numerous opportunities to incorporate mindfulness. Consider starting meetings with a few minutes of collective breathing. Encourage everyone to close their eyes, take deep breaths, and focus on the present. This practice can help create a calmer, more focused environment, reducing the stress and anxiety often accompanying workplace interactions. Additionally, taking mindful breaks throughout the workday can be incredibly beneficial. Step away from your desk, take a few deep breaths, and focus on your surroundings. These short pauses can refresh your mind and improve your overall productivity.

Mindfulness can also enhance social interactions. When conversing with someone, practice active listening. Focus on the speaker without planning your response or letting your mind wander. Notice their tone, expressions, and body language. This practice improves listening skills, fosters deeper connections, and reduces social anxiety. Mindful communication involves speaking with intention and awareness. Before responding, take a moment to consider your words and their impact. This cautious approach to communication can help you express yourself more clearly and compassionately, reducing misunderstandings and conflicts.

Maintaining mindfulness throughout the day can be challenging, but practical tips can help. Setting reminders on your digital devices can prompt you to take mindful pauses. For instance, you can set an alarm to remind you to take a few deep breaths every hour. A mindful morning routine can also set a positive tone for the day. Start your morning with a few minutes of conscious breathing, a short meditation, or a mindful walk. This practice can help you approach the day with a sense of calm and focus. Mindfulness prompts, such as rings or alarms, can serve as gentle reminders to stay present. These prompts can be visual cues in your environment, like a sticky note on your computer, or auditory signals, like a gentle chime on your phone.

Interactive Element: Mindfulness Prompts Checklist

Create a checklist of mindfulness prompts to integrate into your daily routine. Include items like:

- mindful eating
- mindful walking
- mindful cleaning
- mindful breaks
- active listening
- mindful communication

Use this checklist to remind yourself to practice mindfulness throughout the day and reflect on how these practices impact your stress and anxiety levels.

Incorporating mindfulness into daily activities transforms routine tasks into opportunities for meditation and presence. By practicing mindful eating, walking, and cleaning, you can create moments of calm and reduce anxiety. Bringing mindfulness into work settings and social interactions enhances focus and connection, making these experiences more fulfilling. Practical tips like setting reminders and creating a mindful morning routine can help you maintain mindfulness throughout the day, supporting your mental health and well-being.

USING MEDITATION APPS EFFECTIVELY

Meditation apps have become a valuable tool for many people seeking to incorporate mindfulness into their daily routines. They offer accessibility and convenience, making it easier to practice mindfulness wherever you are. Whether at home, commuting, or taking a break at work, these apps provide guided sessions tailored to various needs and levels. The structured approach of guided sessions can be particularly helpful for beginners who may find it challenging to meditate independently. Moreover, the flexibility of choosing different lengths and types of meditation allows you to fit mindfulness practices into your busy schedule, even if you only have a few minutes to spare.

When selecting the proper meditation app, several criteria can help you find one that fits your needs:

- First, consider the variety of meditation types and lengths offered. An app that provides many options—from short, quick sessions to longer, more in-depth practices—can adapt to your changing needs and preferences.
- Additionally, the user interface and ease of use are crucial. An intuitive app with a clean, user-friendly design will make your meditation experience more enjoyable and less frustrating.
- Look for additional features such as sleep aids, progress tracking, and customizable reminders. These features can enhance your practice by helping you monitor your progress, establish a routine, and address issues like insomnia or stress.

To make the most of the features provided by meditation apps, start by setting daily reminders for your meditation sessions. Many apps allow you to schedule notifications that prompt you to take a few moments to meditate. These reminders can help you build a consistent practice, even on the busiest days. Explore the different meditation styles the app offers to find what resonates with you. Whether it's mindful breathing, body scans, or loving-kindness meditation, trying various techniques can keep your practice fresh and engaging. Progress tracking features can also be incredibly motivating. You can see tangible evidence of your efforts paying off by monitoring your meditation streaks and noticing improvements in your mood or stress levels.

Consider the story of Lisa, a busy parent who found calm through 10-minute guided sessions on a meditation app. With a hectic schedule juggling work and family responsibilities, Lisa struggled to find time for self-care. She decided to try a meditation app that offered short, guided sessions. Each morning, Lisa spent just 10 minutes meditating before starting her day. This brief practice helped her feel more centered and less overwhelmed, making it easier to handle the demands of her busy life. The app's soothing voice and gentle guidance provided a much-needed respite, and Lisa began to look forward to these peaceful moments each day.

Another example is Dan, a student who used sleep meditation features to improve his rest. Dan often found himself lying awake at night, his mind racing about exams, assignments, and social pressures. Dan listened to these sessions before bed after downloading a meditation app with specialized sleep meditations. The calming narratives and relaxation techniques helped quiet his mind and prepare his body for sleep. Over time, Dan noticed significant improvements in his sleep quality, enhancing his focus and performance during the day. The app's progress tracking also allowed Dan to see how his sleep patterns improved, providing further motivation to continue his practice.

These stories illustrate the transformative power of meditation apps. By offering accessibility, convenience, and a range of guided sessions, these apps make incorporating mindfulness into your daily life easier. Whether you're a busy parent, a student, or anyone looking to manage stress and improve well-being, meditation apps provide a valuable resource to support your mental health journey.

As we wrap up this chapter, remember that mindfulness and meditation are not about achieving perfection but making progress. The tools and techniques discussed here will help you find moments of peace and clarity amid life's chaos. In the next chapter, we will explore strategies for managing anxiety at work, providing practical tips to help you stay calm and focused professionally.

CHAPTER 6
MANAGING ANXIETY
AT WORK

I remember sitting at my desk, my heart racing and palms sweating, just minutes before an important meeting. The pressure to perform, the fear of judgment, and the overwhelming need to appear competent all converged, leaving me paralyzed with anxiety. This feeling is all too familiar for many professionals—meetings, whether routine or high-stakes, can be a significant source of stress and anxiety. However, with the proper techniques, it is possible to approach these situations with a sense of calm and confidence.

TECHNIQUES TO STAY CALM DURING MEETINGS

Preparation is vital when it comes to managing anxiety before a meeting. One effective strategy is to practice deep breathing exercises before entering the meeting room. Find a quiet space, close your eyes, and take slow, deep breaths. Inhale deeply through your nose, hold for a few seconds, and then exhale slowly through your mouth. This simple exercise activates your parasympathetic nervous system, helping to reduce stress and promote a sense of calm.

Another essential preparation technique is reviewing the agenda and preparing notes. Familiarize yourself with the key topics to discuss, and jot down any points you want to contribute. Understanding the meeting's structure and your role can alleviate anxiety and boost your confidence. Visualization techniques can also be beneficial. Take a few moments to close your eyes and imagine a successful meeting. Visualize yourself speaking confidently, engaging with colleagues, and contributing valuable insights. This mental rehearsal can create a positive mindset and reduce anxiety.

Setting a positive intention for the meeting can further enhance your preparedness. Before the meeting begins, take a moment to set a clear, positive intention. This could be something like, "I will stay focused and present," or "I will contribute thoughtfully and confidently." By setting a positive intention, you align your mindset with your goals, making it easier to navigate the meeting with a sense of purpose and calm.

Maintaining a sense of calm once you're in the meeting requires deliberate effort. Focus on slow, intentional breathing to stay grounded. Whenever you feel your anxiety rising, take a deep breath and exhale slowly. This helps to anchor your mind and body, preventing anxiety from taking over. Engaging in active listening is another powerful technique. By entirely focusing on what others are saying, you stay present and reduce the tendency to get lost in anxious thoughts. Active listening involves making eye contact, nodding to show understanding, and asking clarifying questions when needed. This helps you stay present and fosters better communication and collaboration.

Using grounding techniques can also be beneficial during the meeting. Grounding involves focusing on physical sensations to anchor yourself in the present moment. For example, feel your feet firmly planted on the ground or notice the texture of the chair you're sitting on. These simple actions can help you stay connected to the here and now, reducing the intensity of anxious thoughts.

After the meeting, taking time for post-meeting reflection is crucial for managing anxiety and improving future performance. Journaling your thoughts and feelings about the meeting can provide valuable insights. Write down what went well and any areas where you felt challenged. This reflection helps you identify patterns and areas for improvement. Practicing self-compassion during this process is essential. Acknowledge your efforts and avoid harsh self-criticism. Remember that everyone experiences anxiety and makes mistakes. Treat yourself with kindness and recognize the progress you've made.

Performance anxiety, particularly related to public speaking, is a common challenge in meetings. To manage this anxiety, rehearse critical points and potential questions beforehand. This preparation can boost your confidence and reduce the fear of being caught off guard. Using positive affirmations before speaking can also be empowering. Repeat phrases like, "I am prepared and capable" or "I speak confidently and clearly." These affirmations can counteract negative self-talk and build a positive mindset. Making eye contact during the meeting can further enhance your confidence. Eye contact fosters connection and shows that you are engaged and present. It also helps to reduce feelings of isolation and self-consciousness.

Interactive Element: Post-Meeting Reflection Journal

Create a journal dedicated to post-meeting reflections. After each meeting, write down your thoughts and feelings for a few minutes. Include sections for what went well, areas for improvement, and any positive affirmations or intentions you set. This practice helps you process your experiences and provides a valuable record of your progress and growth.

Incorporating these techniques into your routine can transform your meeting approach and reduce anxiety. Preparation, in-meeting strategies, and post-meeting reflection are crucial in managing anxiety and building confidence. With practice and persistence, you can navigate meetings with a sense of calm and purpose, enhancing your professional performance and overall well-being.

MANAGING WORKLOAD WITHOUT OVERWHELM

Balancing a heavy workload can often feel like juggling too many balls at once, with the constant fear that one will drop. Prioritizing tasks effectively can make a significant difference in managing this load. One of the most effective strategies is using the Eisenhower Matrix. This tool helps you categorize tasks by urgency and importance. Tasks that are both urgent and important should be tackled first. Important but not urgent tasks can be scheduled for later. Urgent but unimportant tasks can be delegated, and urgent and important tasks can be eliminated. This straightforward framework allows you to focus on what truly matters, reducing the sense of overwhelm.

Daily to-do lists with ranked priorities are another practical way to manage your workload. Start each day by listing all the tasks you need to accomplish. Then, rank them in order of importance and urgency. This gives you a clear roadmap for the day and helps you stay focused and organized. As you complete each task, crossing it off your list provides a slight sense of accomplishment that can keep you motivated throughout the day.

Time management techniques can further help prevent overwhelm. Time blocking is an effective method for scheduling specific times for different tasks. By allocating dedicated blocks of time for each task, you create a structured routine that can boost productivity and reduce stress. The Pomodoro Technique is another helpful strategy. This involves working in focused intervals, typically 25 minutes, followed by a short break. After four intervals, take a more extended break. This method encourages deep work while preventing burnout. Limiting multitasking is also crucial. While it may feel like you're accomplishing more, multitasking often leads to decreased efficiency and increased stress. Focus on one task at a time to enhance productivity and reduce anxiety.

Setting healthy boundaries is essential for managing your workload and reducing anxiety. Learning to say no to additional tasks when necessary is a vital skill. It's essential to recognize your limits and communicate them effectively. Setting clear expectations with colleagues and supervisors can also help. Let them know your current workload and discuss realistic deadlines. This open communication fosters a supportive work environment and helps prevent misunderstandings. Allocating time for breaks and self-care is equally important. Schedule regular breaks throughout your day to recharge and avoid burnout. These breaks can be as simple as a short walk, a few minutes of deep breathing, or a quick stretch. Prioritizing self-care ensures you have the energy and focus to tackle your tasks effectively.

Delegation and collaboration are powerful tools for managing workload. Identifying tasks that can be delegated is the first step. Consider which tasks can be handled by others and delegate them accordingly. This frees up your time to focus on higher-priority tasks. Communicating effectively with team members is critical to successful delegation. Clearly explain the task, provide necessary resources, and set expectations for completion. Building a collaborative work environment can also make a significant difference. Encourage teamwork and open communication. When team members support each other, it lightens the load and creates a more positive work atmosphere.

Consider the story of David, a project manager who felt overwhelmed by his workload. By implementing the Eisenhower Matrix, he could prioritize his tasks more effectively. He also started using the Pomodoro Technique, which improved his focus and productivity. Additionally, David learned to set boundaries by communicating his workload with his supervisor and delegating tasks to his team. These changes not only reduced his anxiety but also enhanced his overall performance.

It's important to remember that managing your workload is about being more productive and creating a sustainable routine that supports your mental well-being. By prioritizing tasks, managing your time effectively, setting healthy boundaries, and fostering collaboration, you can reduce overwhelm and navigate your workday more easily and confidently.

QUICK DESK EXERCISES TO REDUCE STRESS

When you're feeling the pressure build at work, quick desk exercises can provide immediate relief and help you regain focus. Physical exercises are a great place to start.

Neck Roll

One simple yet effective exercise is the neck roll:

1. Sit straight, relax your shoulders, and gently roll your head in a circular motion.
2. Start by bringing your right ear to your right shoulder, then let your chin drop to your chest, and finally, bring your left ear to your left shoulder. Repeat this motion a few times in each direction.

Neck rolls help release tension and increase blood flow to your brain, making you feel more relaxed and alert.

Shoulder Shrug

Another beneficial exercise is the shoulder shrug:

1. Raise your shoulders to your ears, hold them for a few seconds, and then release them back down.
2. Repeat this several times.

This exercise helps relieve shoulder and upper back tension, especially if you've been sitting for long periods.

Desk Yoga

Desk yoga poses can also be very effective. The seated cat-cow pose is a gentle way to stretch your back and improve flexibility:

1. Sit on the edge of your chair with your feet flat on the
   floor.
2. Place your hands on your knees.
3. As you inhale, arch your back and look up, creating a slight
   curve in your spine.
4. As you exhale, round your back and tuck your chin to your
   chest.
5. Repeat this sequence a few times.

Another great pose is the seated twist:

1. Sit straight, place your right hand on the back of your chair,
   and twist your torso to the right.
2. Hold for a few breaths, and then switch sides.

This twist helps to release tension in your spine and improve your
posture.

Breathing Exercises

Breathing exercises are another powerful tool for reducing anxiety
right at your desk. The 4-7-8 breathing technique is simple yet
effective:

1. Sit comfortably, close your eyes, and inhale through your nose
   for a count of four.
2. Hold your breath for a count of seven, and then exhale through
   your mouth for eight.

This technique helps to activate your parasympathetic nervous system,
promoting relaxation and reducing stress.

Another helpful breathing exercise is alternate nostril breathing:

1. Close your right nostril with your thumb and inhale deeply
   through your left nostril.
2. Then close your left nostril with your ring finger, release your
   right nostril, and exhale through it.

3. Repeat this pattern for a few minutes to balance your nervous system and calm your mind.

Desk Mindfulness

Mindfulness exercises can also be done at your desk to help you stay grounded. A straightforward practice is mindful breathing:

1. Close your eyes and focus on your breath for a few minutes.
2. Notice the sensation of the air entering and leaving your nostrils, the rise and fall of your chest, and the rhythm of your breath.

This practice helps to anchor your mind in the present moment, reducing anxiety and improving focus.

Sensory focus is another effective mindfulness exercise:

1. Take a moment to notice the textures, sounds, or smells around you.
2. Feel the texture of your desk, listen to the hum of your computer, or notice the scent of your coffee.

Engaging your senses helps to ground you in the present moment and reduce the intensity of anxious thoughts.

Stress-Relief Tools

Using stress-relief tools and gadgets at your desk can provide quick and effective relief:

- Stress balls or fidget spinners can help release nervous energy and keep your hands occupied. Squeezing a stress ball or spinning a fidget spinner can provide a physical outlet for stress, helping you feel more relaxed and focused.
- Aromatherapy diffusers with calming scents like lavender or chamomile can create a soothing environment. The gentle aroma can help to reduce stress and promote a sense of calm.

- Desk plants can also contribute to a calming atmosphere. Plants like succulents or small potted plants improve air quality and provide a visual reminder of nature, which can be calming and grounding.

Interactive Element: Desk Exercise Routine

Create a simple desk exercise routine with physical exercises, breathing techniques, and mindfulness practices. Write down the exercises, how to perform them, and the benefits they provide. Keep this routine handy at your desk whenever you need a quick break to reduce stress and refocus your mind.

BUILDING A SUPPORT NETWORK AT WORK

In the hustle and bustle of the modern workplace, having a support network can be invaluable for managing anxiety. Identifying supportive colleagues starts with recognizing those who are empathetic and understanding. These people genuinely listen, offer constructive feedback, and create a safe space for open conversations. They might be the ones who check in on you during stressful times or provide a helping hand without being asked. Initiating conversations and building rapport with these colleagues can lay the foundation for a strong support network. Start small—chat over a coffee break or discuss common interests. These interactions, though seemingly minor, can foster deeper connections over time. Engaging in team-building activities also helps. Whether participating in a team lunch, a group project, or company-sponsored events, these activities provide opportunities to bond outside the usual work tasks, strengthening your relationships and creating a more cohesive team.

Creating or joining peer support groups at work can also be a game-changer. These groups offer a structured way to share experiences, provide mutual support, and discuss strategies for managing stress and anxiety. Organizing regular meet-ups for stress relief can be as simple as setting aside 30 minutes once a week to discuss challenges and triumphs. These sessions can be informal, like a "coffee and chat" break, or more structured, with specific topics or activities. Collaborating on wellness initiatives or mindfulness sessions can further enhance the support system. For example, organizing group meditation sessions or wellness challenges can provide a collective experience of stress relief and personal growth. These initiatives benefit the participants and contribute to a more supportive and resilient workplace culture.

Utilizing workplace resources is another effective way to build and maintain a support network. Many companies offer Employee Assistance Programs (EAPs) that provide confidential counseling services, mental health resources, and support for personal and professional issues. Accessing these programs can provide valuable tools and guidance for managing anxiety. Participating in wellness programs offered by your employer can also be beneficial. These programs often include activities like yoga, fitness classes, and stress management workshops, providing structured opportunities to improve your well-being. Seeking mentorship or guidance from supervisors can also be incredibly supportive. A good mentor can offer advice, share experiences, and provide a different perspective on challenges, helping you navigate the complexities of the workplace more easily.

Promoting a culture of support within your workplace can amplify these benefits. Encouraging open communication about mental health is a crucial first step. Normalizing conversations about stress, anxiety, and mental health challenges can reduce stigma and create a more inclusive environment. Recognizing and celebrating team achievements also fosters a positive atmosphere. Acknowledging your colleagues' hard work and successes can boost morale and build a sense of collective accomplishment. Advocating for mental health awareness and support initiatives can further strengthen the workplace culture. This could involve organizing mental health awareness events, distributing educational materials, or working with HR to implement supportive policies and programs. These actions demonstrate a commitment to mental well-being and encourage others to prioritize their health.

We've covered identifying supportive colleagues, creating peer support groups, utilizing workplace resources, and promoting a supportive culture. The next chapter will delve into the power of social connections and how fostering meaningful relationships can further enhance your ability to manage anxiety and improve overall well-being.

SHARE YOUR THOUGHTS, MAKE A DIFFERENCE

We rise by lifting others. –Robert Ingersoll

The Power of Your Voice

Helping others feels good, doesn't it? When we lift someone up, we rise, too. Today, you have a special opportunity to do just that.

Are you on a journey to manage anxiety and improve your well-being? My goal with *Practical Guide to Rewire Your Anxious Brain* is to make that journey smoother for everyone. But I can't do it alone! I need your help to reach more people who might be searching for the same answers you've found.

Reviews are like a guiding light for people looking for the right book. Sharing your thoughts can help someone else take a step forward in their journey. Your review could help…

- one more person feel less overwhelmed by anxiety.
- one more reader discover new ways to boost their mental and physical health.
- one more individual find peace and balance in their daily life.
- one more person learn how to build lasting resilience.

If you'd like to make a difference, scan the QR code below or follow the link to leave your review:

[https://www.amazon.com/review/review-your-purchases/?asin=B0DLKSPNNW]

Thank you for taking the time to share your experience and for helping others find their way!

Warmly,

Eva Keene

CHAPTER 7

SOCIAL ANXIETY AND CONNECTIONS

I remember standing in the corner of a crowded room, clutching my drink like a lifeline. My heart raced, my palms sweated, and my mind was whirling with anxious thoughts. The fear of judgment and rejection loomed large, making it almost impossible to engage in conversation. If you've ever felt this way, you're not alone. Social anxiety can be incredibly isolating and overwhelming, but understanding its roots and learning effective strategies can help you navigate social events with greater ease.

OVERCOMING FEAR OF SOCIAL EVENTS

Social anxiety often stems from a deep-seated fear of judgment or rejection. You might worry that others scrutinize your every move, waiting for you to slip up. This fear can lead to negative self-perception, where you see yourself as inadequate or unworthy. Past traumatic social experiences, such as being bullied or humiliated, can exacerbate these feelings, reinforcing the belief that social situations are dangerous and should be avoided. These underlying causes create a vicious cycle, where the fear of social events leads to avoidance, reinforcing the fear.

One effective way to break this cycle is through exposure therapy. This method involves gradually facing your social fears in a controlled and systematic way. Start with low-stakes interactions, like making small talk with a cashier or asking a colleague about their weekend. These brief exchanges can help build your confidence and reduce anxiety. As you become more comfortable, the complexity and size of social settings gradually increase. Attend small gatherings with close friends before moving on to larger events with unfamiliar people. Keeping a progress journal can be incredibly helpful in tracking your improvements and identifying patterns. Write down each social interaction, how you felt before and after, and any positive outcomes. This record can be a powerful reminder of your progress and motivate you to keep going.

Cognitive behavioral strategies can also be highly effective in managing social anxiety. Start by identifying and disputing irrational beliefs that fuel your anxiety. For example, if you find yourself thinking, "Everyone is judging me," challenge this thought by asking, "What evidence do I have for this belief?" and "Is it possible that people are more focused on themselves than on me?"

Practicing positive self-talk and affirmations before social events can also boost your confidence. Repeat phrases like, "I am worthy of connection" or "I can handle this situation" to counteract negative self-perception. Visualization is another powerful tool. Before attending a social event, spend a few minutes visualizing a successful interaction. Picture yourself engaging in conversation, feeling calm and confident.

This mental rehearsal can reduce anxiety and increase your chances of having a positive experience.

Managing anxiety in real-time during social events requires practical, actionable strategies. Deep breathing exercises can help you stay calm and centered. When you feel your anxiety rising, take a moment to focus on your breath. Inhale deeply through your nose, hold for a few seconds, and exhale slowly through your mouth. This simple practice can activate your body's relaxation response and reduce anxiety.

Setting small, achievable social goals for each event can also make a big difference. Instead of aiming to talk to everyone in the room, set a goal to have a meaningful conversation with just one or two people. This approach can make social events feel more manageable and less overwhelming. Bringing a supportive friend along for encouragement can provide additional comfort. Having someone you trust by your side can make it easier to navigate social situations and reduce feelings of isolation.

Reflection Exercise: Social Anxiety Progress Journal

Create a progress journal to track your experiences with social anxiety. After each social event, take a few minutes to write about how you felt before and after, what strategies you used, and any positive outcomes. Reflect on any improvements you notice over time. This journal can help you identify patterns, celebrate small victories, and stay motivated to overcome social anxiety.

Understanding the roots of social anxiety and implementing these strategies can help you face social events with greater confidence. By gradually exposing yourself to social situations, challenging negative thoughts, and using practical techniques to manage anxiety in real time, you can break the cycle of fear and avoidance. Remember, progress may be slow, but each step you take brings you closer to feeling more comfortable and connected in social settings.

STRATEGIES TO REBUILD YOUR SOCIAL LIFE

Assessing your current social networks can be an enlightening first step in rebuilding your social life. Grab a piece of paper or open a digital document and map your relationships and social circles:

- Who are the people you interact with regularly?
- Categorize them into different groups like family, friends, colleagues, and acquaintances.
- As you jot down these names, take a moment to reflect on the nature of each relationship. Identify which connections feel supportive and uplifting and which leave you feeling drained or anxious.

This exercise can help you see where to focus your efforts and where gaps might be filled. Setting goals for expanding your social networks becomes easier when you have a clear picture of your current situation. Decide whether you want to deepen existing relationships, reconnect with old friends, or meet new people. Having specific goals can give you direction and make the process less overwhelming.

Finding and joining social groups or clubs that align with your interests can be a game-changer. Start by researching local clubs and organizations. Look for book clubs, sports teams, hobby groups, or volunteer organizations that match your passions. Many communities have bulletin boards, websites, or social media pages listing local events and groups. Attending meetups and community events can also open new doors. These gatherings are designed to bring people together around shared interests, making initiating conversations and forming connections easier. Online platforms like Meetup and Facebook groups offer another excellent resource. These platforms allow you to search for groups based on your interests and location, making it easy to find like-minded individuals. Once you join a group, be proactive in attending events and participating in discussions. The more you engage, the more likely you are to build meaningful connections.

Building and nurturing new friendships requires effort and genuine interest in others. When you meet someone new, take the initiative to start a conversation. Ask open-ended questions and show genuine curiosity about their life and interests. People appreciate when others are interested in them, which can help establish a connection. Following up after initial meetings is crucial for building rapport. Send a message or call to express that you enjoyed the conversation and would like to meet again. Regular social activities can strengthen these new bonds. Whether it's inviting someone for coffee, organizing a game night, or planning a group hike, regular interactions can turn acquaintances into friends. Consistency is key, so stay in touch and show up for the people you want to build relationships with.

Rebuilding your social life comes with its own set of challenges. You may face rejection and setbacks, which can be disheartening. It's important to remember that not every interaction will lead to a lasting friendship, and that's okay. Focus on the positive experiences and learn from the less successful ones. Managing time and energy for social activities can also be challenging, especially if you have a busy schedule. Prioritize social interactions that bring you joy and align with your goals. It's okay to say no to events or activities that feel draining or overwhelming. Balancing your social life with other responsibilities requires mindful planning. Use a calendar or planner to schedule social activities alongside your work and personal commitments. This way, you can ensure that you have time for everything without feeling stretched too thin.

Navigating the complexities of social life can be daunting, but with thoughtful strategies and genuine effort, you can build a supportive and enriching social network. Assessing your current relationships, joining new groups, actively nurturing friendships, and overcoming challenges are all part of the process. Remember, building a social life takes time, and it's okay to take small steps. Each interaction, each new connection, brings you closer to a fuller, more connected life.

CULTIVATING MEANINGFUL RELATIONSHIPS

Meaningful relationships are the bedrock of emotional well-being and resilience. They are characterized by trust and mutual respect, where both parties feel safe and valued. Trust is built over time through consistent actions and honesty. When you trust someone, you feel confident they have your best interests at heart, creating a secure foundation for the relationship. Mutual respect involves valuing each other's opinions, feelings, and boundaries. It's about recognizing the inherent worth of the other person and treating them accordingly. Emotional support and understanding are also vital qualities. In a meaningful relationship, you feel supported during tough times and understood without judgment. This emotional safety net helps you navigate life's challenges with greater ease. Lastly, shared values and interests bind people together. When you connect with someone who shares your passions and principles, the bond deepens, and the relationship becomes more fulfilling. These qualities are essential for mental health as they provide a sense of belonging and security, which can buffer against stress and anxiety.

Communication is the lifeblood of any meaningful relationship. Active listening and empathetic responses are crucial for deepening connections. When someone speaks, give them your full attention. Put away distractions and focus on their words, body language, and emotions. Reflect on what you hear to show that you understand. For instance, "It sounds like you're feeling frustrated because of what happened at work." This not only validates their feelings but also fosters a deeper connection. Expressing gratitude and appreciation regularly can also strengthen relationships. A simple "thank you" or a note of appreciation can significantly make the other person feel valued.

Another essential skill is resolving conflicts constructively. Conflicts are inevitable, but how you handle them makes all the difference. Approach disagreements with a problem-solving mindset rather than a confrontational one. Use "I" statements to express your feelings without blaming others. For example, "I feel hurt when my concerns are dismissed" instead of "You never listen to me." This approach helps in finding solutions without damaging the relationship.

Setting healthy boundaries is vital for maintaining the integrity of any relationship. Recognize and clearly communicate your limits. Let others know what is acceptable and what is not. For instance, if you need alone time to recharge, communicate this to your friends or family. Saying no without guilt is part of setting boundaries. It's okay to decline invitations or requests that you don't have the capacity for. Remember, taking care of your mental health is not selfish; it's necessary. Maintaining a balance between giving and receiving is also crucial. Relationships should be reciprocal. If you find yourself constantly giving and never receiving, it might be time to reassess the dynamics. Healthy boundaries ensure that both parties feel respected and valued.

Maintaining and strengthening relationships over time involves consistent effort. Scheduling regular check-ins and quality time can keep the connection strong. Whether it's a weekly phone call, a monthly coffee date, or a quick text to say hello, these small gestures show that you care. Celebrating milestones and achievements together also strengthens bonds. Be there for each other's big moments, whether a birthday, a promotion, or a personal achievement. Sharing in these celebrations reinforces the positive aspects of the relationship. Sharing activities and hobbies can provide common ground and create lasting memories. Whether hiking, cooking, or playing a sport together, these activities deepen the connection and make the relationship more enjoyable.

Building meaningful relationships takes time and effort, but the rewards are immense. Trust, mutual respect, emotional support, and shared values create a strong foundation. Effective communication, setting healthy boundaries, and consistently maintaining the relationship will ensure that it thrives. These relationships provide emotional stability and support, which are crucial for mental health and resilience.

THE ROLE OF COMMUNITY IN ANXIETY MANAGEMENT

Imagine feeling a sense of belonging, knowing that people around you genuinely care about your well-being. This is the power of community support in managing anxiety. Community can significantly reduce feelings of isolation and loneliness, which are often exacerbated by anxiety. When you are part of a community, you are surrounded by people who understand your struggles and can offer practical and emotional support. This sense of belonging and purpose can be incredibly grounding, providing a stable foundation to navigate life's challenges.

Finding and building a supportive community starts with identifying groups that align with your values and interests. Think about what matters most to you and what activities you enjoy. Whether it's a hobby, a cause, or a shared experience, these can all be gateways to finding like-minded individuals. Participating in local events and volunteer opportunities is a great way to meet people who share your passions. Volunteering helps others and gives you a sense of purpose and connection. Additionally, leveraging online communities can provide a broader network of support. Platforms like Reddit, Facebook, and specialized forums offer spaces where you can connect with others who understand your experiences and can provide advice and encouragement.

Engaging in community activities actively helps to build connections and reduce anxiety. Attending community gatherings and social events, even if it's just occasionally, can help you feel more integrated and less isolated. Look for events that interest you, whether it's a local fair, a hobby club meeting, or a cultural festival. Joining support groups for individuals with similar experiences can be particularly beneficial. These groups provide a safe space to share your struggles and triumphs without fear of judgment. Contributing to community projects and initiatives also fosters a sense of belonging. Whether it's a neighborhood clean-up, a charity run, or a community garden, being part of a collective effort can create strong bonds and reduce feelings of isolation.

Sustaining community involvement requires regular participation and a balance with your personal needs. Set a schedule that includes regular community activities, but be mindful not to over-commit. Consistency is key, but listening to your needs and taking breaks when necessary is essential. Encourage others to join and build community together. Invite friends, family, or coworkers to participate in community events with you. This strengthens your support network and fosters a culture of connection and support. Remember, building a community is a two-way street. Be open to offering support and receiving it. The more you engage, the more rewarding your community experience will be.

Building a supportive community can be transformative for managing anxiety. It reduces isolation, provides practical and emotional support, and fosters a sense of belonging and purpose. By actively finding and engaging in communities that align with your values and interests, you can create a network of connections that support your mental well-being. Sustaining these connections requires regular participation and a balance with your personal needs, but the benefits are well worth the effort. In the next chapter, we will explore digital detox and technology's role in managing anxiety, providing additional tools to support your mental health and well-being.

CHAPTER 8
DIGITAL DETOX AND TECHNOLOGY

One evening, I endlessly scrolled through social media, jumping from one app to another. Hours passed unnoticed, and as the night turned into early morning, I felt drained and restless. The constant barrage of notifications, the need to stay updated, and the comparisons to others' seemingly perfect lives left me feeling anxious and disconnected. It was then that I realized the dual nature of technology—how it could be both a blessing and a curse.

UNDERSTANDING THE DOUBLE-EDGED SWORD OF TECHNOLOGY

Technology has revolutionized our lives in countless ways, offering unprecedented convenience and connectivity. It's easier to imagine a world with immediate access to information from the internet. Whether looking for the latest news, researching a topic, or learning a new skill, the information available at your fingertips is unparalleled. Educational resources, from online courses to instructional videos, have democratized learning, enabling anyone with an internet connection to acquire new knowledge and skills.

Technology has also transformed communication. Social media platforms and messaging apps allow us to stay connected with friends and family, regardless of distance. These tools enable real-time conversations, video calls, and sharing moments that would otherwise be missed. For many, especially those living far from loved ones, these platforms provide a lifeline of support and connection. Online communities and support groups have flourished, offering spaces where individuals with shared interests or challenges can come together, share experiences, and provide mutual support.

Productivity tools have streamlined work and personal tasks, making it easier to manage our busy lives. Calendar apps, task managers, and collaboration platforms help us stay organized, meet deadlines, and work efficiently. These tools can reduce stress by providing structure and clarity, allowing us to focus on what truly matters.

However, the very technology that offers these benefits can also be a source of stress and anxiety. Social media, for instance, often fosters a culture of comparison. Scrolling through curated images and highlighting reels of other people's lives makes it easy to feel inadequate or left out. This phenomenon, known as FOMO (fear of missing out), can exacerbate feelings of anxiety and dissatisfaction.

Another significant drawback is information overload. The constant influx of news, messages, and updates can be overwhelming. Notifications demand our attention, pulling us away from tasks and reducing our ability to concentrate. This perpetual alertness can lead to mental fatigue and increased stress levels. The irony is that while technology aims to make our lives easier, the constant connectivity can lead to a sense of always being "on," never fully able to disconnect and relax.

Moreover, the rise of digital communication has led to a decline in face-to-face interactions. While online connections are valuable, they can only partially replace the depth and richness of in-person relationships. The lack of physical presence and non-verbal cues can lead to misunderstandings and isolation. This decreased social interaction can contribute to feelings of loneliness and depression.

Sleep disturbances are another common issue linked to excessive technology use. The blue light emitted by screens can interfere with melatonin production, the hormone responsible for regulating sleep. Late-night scrolling or binge-watching can disrupt your sleep patterns, leading to poor sleep quality and increased anxiety. A good night's sleep is crucial for emotional regulation and overall well-being, and technology's interference with sleep can have far-reaching effects on mental health.

Finding a balance between technology's benefits and drawbacks is crucial. Start by identifying your technology usage patterns. Take note of how often you check your phone, the apps you use most frequently, and when you're most likely to engage with technology. Setting intentional goals for your technology use can help you regain control. Decide when and how you want to use technology and establish boundaries to prevent overuse.

Recognizing signs of technology overuse is also essential. These can include feelings of anxiety or restlessness when away from your devices, neglecting in-person relationships, and experiencing physical symptoms like eye strain or sleep disturbances. By being aware of these signs, you can take proactive steps to address them.

Research has shown the dual nature of technology's impact on mental health. Studies on social media use have found that while it can enhance connectivity, it can also increase feelings of anxiety and depression, particularly among heavy users. One case study highlights an individual who balanced technology use by setting specific times for social media and incorporating tech-free periods into their day. This approach reduced their anxiety and improved their overall well-being. Statistics on screen time reveal that excessive use is linked to reduced sleep quality and productivity, underscoring the importance of mindful technology use.

Interactive Element: Technology Usage Reflection Exercise

Take a few moments to reflect on your technology usage. Write down the following:

- how much time you spend on different devices and apps
- how it makes you feel
- any negative impacts you've noticed on your mental health

Identify areas where you can set boundaries or reduce usage. This exercise can help you gain clarity and take the first steps toward a healthier relationship with technology.

CRAFTING A DIGITAL DETOX PLAN

A digital detox is a deliberate break from digital devices to reduce stress, improve focus, enhance face-to-face social interactions, and improve sleep quality. In today's hyper-connected world, our reliance on technology can become overwhelming. Constant notifications, endless scrolling, and the pressure to stay updated can take a toll on our mental health. A digital detox helps create a buffer, allowing you to reconnect with the present moment and the people around you.

Follow these steps to create a personalized digital detox plan:

1. Assess your current digital habits.
2. Look closely at how much time you spend on your devices each day.
3. Identify which apps or activities consume most of your time.
4. Are you constantly checking social media? Do you find yourself lost in a sea of emails? Understanding your habits is the first step toward making meaningful changes.
5. Once you have a clear picture, set specific goals for reducing screen time. These goals should be realistic and achievable. For example, you could reduce your social media usage by 30 minutes daily or limit email checks to three times daily.

Planning offline activities to replace digital time is crucial. Think about hobbies or interests you've neglected due to screen time. It could be reading a book, walking, or spending time with loved ones. By filling your time with enriching activities, you'll find it easier to step away from your devices. Gradually reducing your dependency on digital devices is another crucial step. Start by implementing small changes, like designating tech-free times during meals or before bed. Over time, increase these periods to create longer stretches of digital-free time.

Practical tips can make your digital detox more successful:

- Designate tech-free zones in your home, such as the bedroom or dining area. This creates physical boundaries that encourage you to disconnect.
- Using apps that monitor and limit screen time can be incredibly helpful. Apps like "Moment" or "Screen Time" provide insights into your usage patterns and help you set limits.
- Engaging in hobbies and activities that don't involve screens is vital. Whether gardening, painting, or playing a musical instrument, these activities provide a fulfilling alternative to screen time.
- Creating a support network can also enhance your detox efforts. Share your goals with friends or family members who can hold you accountable and join you in tech-free activities.

Overcoming challenges during a digital detox requires patience and persistence. Withdrawal symptoms like irritability or boredom are common when reducing screen time. To combat this, plan to engage in offline activities that keep your mind occupied. Managing work-related technology use can be tricky, but setting boundaries is crucial. Allocate specific times for checking emails or attending virtual meetings, and stick to these schedules. Balancing detox with necessary digital engagements means being selective about when and why you use your devices. Prioritize essential tasks and avoid mindless scrolling. Staying motivated through tracking progress and celebrating milestones can provide a sense of accomplishment and reinforce your commitment to the detox. Keep a journal to document your progress, noting any positive changes you experience.

Interactive Element: Digital Detox Challenge

Create a seven-day digital detox challenge for yourself:

1. Set a specific daily goal, such as "No social media after 8 p.m."
   or "Read a book for 30 minutes instead of watching TV."
2. At the end of each day, reflect on your experience. Note any
   challenges, how you felt, and any positive outcomes.

This challenge can help you build healthier digital habits and experience the benefits of a digital detox firsthand.

LEVERAGING TECHNOLOGY FOR MINDFULNESS

Amid our busy lives, finding moments of peace can feel like a luxury. However, technology can be a powerful ally in cultivating mindfulness and reducing anxiety. Mindfulness apps offer guided meditations and exercises that are easily accessible, even if you're always on the go. These apps provide a structured approach to mindfulness, making it easier to incorporate into your daily routine. With customizable reminders and practice schedules, you can set aside specific times for mindfulness practice, ensuring it becomes a consistent part of your life. The diverse types of mindfulness content available—from short breathing exercises to longer meditation sessions—cater to various needs and preferences, allowing you to choose what works best.

- One of the most popular mindfulness apps is Headspace. This app offers a wide range of guided meditations and mindfulness courses to help you manage stress, improve focus, and enhance overall well-being. Whether you're a beginner or an experienced meditator, Headspace provides sessions that cater to different levels and goals.
- Another well-regarded app is Calm, which features sleep stories, breathing exercises, and meditation sessions. Calm's soothing visuals and sounds create a relaxing environment to help you unwind and prepare for restful sleep.
- Insight Timer is another excellent choice, offering a vast library of free meditations and community features. This app allows you to connect with others on a similar mindfulness journey, fostering community and support. Simple Habit is perfect for those with a busy schedule, providing short, on-the-go mindfulness sessions that can be easily integrated into daily life.

Integrating mindfulness apps into your daily routine can be a game-changer. Start by setting daily reminders for mindfulness practice. These reminders prompt you to take a few minutes to focus on your breath or listen to a guided meditation. Beginning your day with a short meditation session can set a positive tone, helping you approach the day's challenges with a calmer mindset. Using mindfulness apps during breaks can also provide quick boosts of relaxation and focus. For example, taking five minutes to practice deep breathing or a body scan meditation during a work break can help you reset and reduce stress. Tracking your progress and reflecting on your mindfulness journey can also be motivating. Many apps offer features that allow you to monitor your meditation streaks and track improvements in mood or stress levels, providing tangible evidence of your progress.

Consider the story of Sophia, a student who used mindfulness apps to manage exam stress. With the pressure of exams looming, Sophia found it difficult to focus and felt overwhelmed by anxiety. She started using Headspace, setting daily reminders for short meditation sessions. Over time, these sessions helped her calm her mind and improve her concentration, making exam preparation more manageable.

Another example is Kevin, a working professional who incorporated mindfulness into his daily commute. He used the Calm app to listen to guided meditations during his train rides, transforming a stressful part of his day into a peaceful experience. This practice not only reduced his anxiety but also helped him arrive at work feeling more centered and focused.

Alyssa, a parent, found solace through bedtime mindfulness stories for her kids using the Calm app. These stories helped her children relax and fall asleep more easily, creating a calmer bedtime routine for the entire family.

Leveraging technology for mindfulness can significantly enhance your ability to manage stress and anxiety. By making mindfulness practices accessible and integrating them into your daily routine, you can create pockets of peace amidst the busyness of life. Whether you're a student managing academic stress, a professional navigating a hectic workday, or a parent seeking calm, mindfulness apps offer practical tools to support your mental well-being. The stories of Sophia, Kevin, and Alyssa illustrate the transformative power of these practices, demonstrating how technology can be a valuable ally in your journey toward a more balanced and fulfilling life.

SETTING HEALTHY BOUNDARIES WITH DIGITAL DEVICES

Setting boundaries with digital devices is vital for your mental health and anxiety management. Without boundaries, it's easy to fall into the trap of technology overuse and dependency. You might find yourself reaching for your phone when you wake up, scrolling through social media during meals, and checking emails late into the night. This constant connectivity can lead to mental fatigue and increased anxiety. By setting clear boundaries, you can prevent technology from taking over your life, allowing you to focus on what truly matters.

One significant benefit of establishing digital boundaries is improved focus and productivity. When you're not constantly interrupted by notifications or tempted to check your phone, you can concentrate better on the task. This increased focus can lead to more efficient work and more significant accomplishments. Additionally, by dedicating specific time to digital use, you can ensure that your job doesn't spill over into your personal life, creating a healthier work-life balance.

Improving personal relationships is another crucial reason to set digital boundaries. When you're not distracted by screens, you can be fully present with your loved ones. Whether having a meal together, engaging in a meaningful conversation, or simply spending quality time, being present without digital interruptions can strengthen your relationships. Your loved ones will appreciate your undivided attention, and you'll find that these moments of genuine connection can significantly enhance your emotional well-being.

To set and maintain healthy digital boundaries, start by creating tech-free times and zones. For example, designate meal times and the bedroom as tech-free areas. This means no phones at the dinner table and no screens before bed. These simple changes can make a significant difference in your ability to disconnect and recharge. Limiting notifications is another effective strategy. Turn off non-essential notifications to reduce constant interruptions. You can also schedule regular digital detox periods, such as one tech-free day per week or a weekend unplugged from devices. Using apps to monitor and limit screen time can help you stay accountable. Apps like Moment or Digital Wellbeing provide insights into your usage patterns and help you set limits.

Balancing digital device use for work and personal life requires clear boundaries. Start by setting specific times for work-related technology use, such as checking emails only during designated hours. Using separate devices for work and personal activities can also help create a physical boundary between the two. For instance, use a work laptop for professional tasks and keep personal activities on your phone or a tablet. Communicating these boundaries with colleagues and family members is essential. Let them know your availability and the times when you'll be offline. This way, they can respect your boundaries and understand that you prioritize your mental well-being.

Maintaining digital boundaries over time can be challenging but crucial for long-term success. Regularly review and adjust your boundaries as needed. Life is dynamic, and what works today might need tweaking tomorrow. Engage in offline activities and hobbies that you enjoy. Whether reading, cooking, exercising, or spending time outdoors, these activities can provide a fulfilling alternative to screen time. Encouraging family and friends to support and join your boundary-setting efforts can also make a significant difference. Everyone on board creates a supportive environment that makes maintaining boundaries easier.

By setting healthy digital boundaries, you create space for meaningful connections, improved focus, and reduced anxiety. These boundaries help you regain control over your technology use, allowing you to live more mindfully and intentionally. Remember, the goal is not to eliminate technology but to use it to enhance your life rather than detract from it. By setting and maintaining these boundaries, you can create a healthier relationship with technology and improve your overall well-being.

As we move forward, we must recognize how integrating physical health strategies can further support your mental well-being. In the next chapter, we'll explore the importance of exercise, nutrition, and sleep in managing anxiety, providing you with additional tools to create a balanced and fulfilling life.

CHAPTER 9

HOLISTIC APPROACHES TO ANXIETY

One afternoon, feeling the weight of a particularly stressful week, I decided to walk in a nearby park. The moment I stepped onto the trail, surrounded by the rustling leaves and chirping birds, I felt a sense of calm wash over me. The anxiety gnawing at my mind began to ease, replaced by a peaceful connection to the natural world. At that moment, I discovered the profound impact that nature could have on my mental well-being.

EMBRACING ECOTHERAPY AND NATURE WALKS

Ecotherapy, also known as nature therapy or green therapy, involves engaging with the natural environment to support mental health. This practice harnesses nature's therapeutic benefits to reduce stress and improve mood. Ecotherapy works by tapping into humans' innate connection with the natural world, providing a sense of grounding and tranquility that is often missing in our fast-paced, technology-driven lives. Spending time outdoors allows your mind and body to reset, enhancing feelings of connectedness and well-being.

Connecting with nature offers a break from the constant stimuli of modern life, allowing your brain to decompress and recover from stress. Walking through a park or sitting by a lake can significantly reduce cortisol levels, the hormone associated with stress. Nature exposure has been shown to lower blood pressure, slow heart rate, and reduce muscle tension, all contributing to a calmer state of mind. Additionally, spending time outdoors promotes physical activity, a powerful tool for anxiety management.

Nature walks are an accessible and effective way to incorporate ecotherapy into your routine. These walks not only reduce stress but also improve focus and cognitive function. The natural environment engages your senses in a way that urban settings often do not, providing a mental break that can lead to increased creativity and problem-solving abilities. When walking through a forest or along a beach, your mind has the space to wander and process thoughts more freely, often leading to new insights and a clearer perspective on challenges.

To make ecotherapy a regular part of your life, start by finding local parks or natural areas where you can walk or sit quietly. Even urban environments often have hidden green spaces that can provide a brief escape from the hustle and bustle. Joining group hikes or nature clubs can also be a great way to stay motivated and meet like-minded individuals who share your interest in nature. If getting out into nature is only sometimes feasible, consider creating a small garden or indoor plant space. Tending to plants can offer similar benefits, providing a calming and grounding activity that connects you to the natural world.

Consider the story of Maria, a corporate professional who found herself overwhelmed by the demands of her job. She began incorporating lunchtime walks in a nearby park, using the time to disconnect from work and reconnect with herself. These brief escapes allowed her to return to the office with a clearer mind and reduced stress, improving her overall productivity and well-being.

Then, there's Jack, a student struggling with the pressures of exams and assignments. He found solace in weekend hikes, immersing himself in the beauty and tranquility of nature. These hikes provided him with a much-needed mental break, helping him focus better during study sessions and manage his anxiety more effectively.

Another inspiring example is Evelyn, a retiree who turned to gardening as a way to find peace and purpose. By cultivating a small garden in her backyard, she created a sanctuary where she could spend time nurturing plants. The physical activity and connection to nature significantly improved her mental health, providing a sense of accomplishment and joy.

Reflection Exercise: Nature Connection Journal

Take a few moments each week to journal about your experiences in nature. Write about where you went, what you saw, and how it made you feel. Reflect on any changes in your mood or stress levels. This practice can help deepen your connection to nature and reinforce its benefits for your mental well-being.

Integrating ecotherapy and nature walks into your life offers a simple yet powerful way to manage anxiety. Regularly connecting with the natural world can reduce stress, improve focus, and enhance your overall sense of well-being. Whether through walks in the park, group hikes, or gardening, nature provides a healing balm for the mind and soul.

YOGA AND STRETCHING FOR ANXIETY RELIEF

Yoga has long been celebrated for its ability to manage anxiety and improve overall mental health. Yoga offers a holistic approach to well-being through physical postures, breathing exercises, and meditation. Practicing yoga engages both your body and mind, enhancing body awareness and emotional regulation. The physical postures, or asanas, help release muscle tension, while the breathing exercises, or pranayama, promote relaxation and reduce stress hormones. Meditation, often incorporated into yoga sessions, helps calm the mind and fosters a sense of inner peace.

One of the key benefits of yoga is its ability to promote relaxation. This is achieved through a combination of mindful movement and focused breathing.

Child's Pose

Child's pose (Balasana) is a simple yet powerful posture that promotes relaxation and grounding:

1. To practice this pose, kneel on the floor, sit back on your heels, and stretch your arms forward, resting your forehead on the mat.

This position gently stretches the back and allows you to focus on your breath, creating a sense of calm and safety.

Legs Up the Wall Pose

Legs up the wall pose (Viparita Karani) is another effective posture for reducing stress and improving circulation:

1. To practice this pose, lie on your back with your legs extended up against a wall.

This inversion helps redirect blood flow, reducing swelling and promoting relaxation. It also encourages the parasympathetic nervous system to activate, which counteracts the stress response.

Cat-Cow Pose

Cat-cow pose (Marjaryasana-Bitilasana) is excellent for releasing tension in the spine:

1. Begin on your hands and knees, with your wrists aligned under your shoulders and your knees under your hips.
2. Inhale as you arch your back, lifting your head and tailbone (cow pose), then exhale as you round your spine, tucking your chin and pelvis (cat pose).

This gentle flow helps improve spinal flexibility and reduces stress held in the back and shoulders.

Corpse Pose

Finally, corpse pose (Savasana) is a practice of deep relaxation and mindfulness:

1. Lie flat on your back with your legs comfortably apart and
   your arms resting at your sides, palms facing up.
2. Close your eyes and focus on your breath, allowing your body
   to relax fully.

This pose helps integrate the benefits of your yoga practice and
provides a moment of complete stillness and peace.

Stretching Exercises

Incorporating stretching exercises into your daily routine can also
significantly reduce anxiety. Neck and shoulder stretches are particularly effective in releasing tension that often accumulates in these areas
due to stress:

1. Gently tilt your head to one side, bringing your ear toward
   your shoulder, and hold for a few breaths before switching
   sides.

This simple stretch can alleviate tightness and promote relaxation.

Hamstring Stretches

Hamstring stretches improve circulation and reduce tension in the
lower body:

1. Sit on the floor with your legs extended in front of you.
2. Slowly reach forward, aiming to touch your toes.
3. Hold this position for a few breaths, feeling the stretch along
   the back of your legs.

This exercise helps reduce physical tension and enhances overall flexibility.

Spinal Twist

Gentle spinal twists are also beneficial for relaxation:

1. Sit on the floor with your legs extended.
2. Bend one knee and place your foot on the opposite side of the extended leg.
3. Twist your torso toward the bent knee, using your arm to deepen the stretch.
4. Hold for a few breaths and repeat on the other side.

Spinal twists help release tension in the back and improve spinal mobility.

To create a sustainable yoga and stretching routine, set aside specific times for practice, such as morning or evening. Consistency is key to reaping the benefits of these exercises. Online yoga classes or apps can provide guidance and structure, making it easier to maintain your practice. Combining yoga and stretching with mindfulness practices can further enhance their effectiveness, creating a comprehensive approach to managing anxiety.

THE BENEFITS OF CREATIVE OUTLETS

There was a time when words seemed to fail me, and my mind was a tangled web of anxiety and stress. During one of these difficult periods, I stumbled upon the transformative power of creative outlets. Engaging in creative activities offers a unique way to manage anxiety. These activities provide an emotional outlet, allowing you to express feelings that words often cannot capture. Whether it's the swipe of a paintbrush, the strum of a guitar, or the crafting of a poem, creative pursuits can significantly reduce stress by redirecting your focus and energy. They enhance self-expression and self-awareness, giving you insights into your inner world and helping you process emotions in a healthy way. The sense of accomplishment and joy that comes from creating something with your own hands can be incredibly uplifting, fostering a positive outlook and boosting self-esteem.

- Art therapy is one of the most effective forms of creative outlets for managing anxiety. Painting, drawing, and sculpting allow you to visually express your emotions, providing a tangible way to release pent-up feelings. The act of creating art engages your mind and hands, diverting your thoughts from anxiety and focusing them on the present moment. This immersion in the creative process can be deeply meditative, promoting relaxation and mental clarity.
- Music therapy is another powerful tool. Playing an instrument, singing, or writing songs can be a cathartic experience. Music allows you to channel your emotions through sound, creating a harmonious outlet for stress and anxiety.
- Writing, whether through journaling, creative writing, or poetry, offers a similar release. Putting your feelings and thoughts down into words can help you make sense of your experiences, providing clarity and perspective.
- Crafting activities like knitting, crocheting, and DIY projects also offer therapeutic benefits. These repetitive, hands-on tasks can be soothing and grounding, helping to calm an anxious mind.

Incorporating creative activities into your daily routine can be a manageable time commitment. Start by setting aside dedicated time for your creative pursuits. Whether it's 15 minutes a day or an hour a week, consistency is vital. Create a designated space for your activities, even if it's just a corner of a room. Having a specific place for your creative work can make it easier to get started and stay focused. Joining creative groups or classes can also provide inspiration and support. Being part of a community of like-minded individuals can enhance your motivation and provide valuable feedback and encouragement.

Consider the story of Anna, an office worker who found herself overwhelmed by the pressures of her job. She decided to take up painting as a way to unwind after work. The simple act of applying color to canvas became a form of meditation for her, allowing her to disconnect from work-related stress and reconnect with herself. She found that painting not only reduced her anxiety but also brought her a sense of joy and fulfillment.

Then, there's Tom, a musician who struggled with anxiety during challenging times. He turned to songwriting, using his music to process his emotions and express his fears and hopes. The act of creating songs provided him with an emotional outlet and helped him navigate his anxiety more effectively.

Lastly, consider Susan, a retiree who discovered the joys of crafting. She took up knitting and DIY projects, finding peace and satisfaction in creating handmade items. These activities kept her mind engaged and provided a sense of purpose and accomplishment.

Interactive Element: Creative Journaling Prompt

Set aside a few minutes each day to journal about your creative activities. Write about what you created, how the process made you feel, and any insights or emotions that emerged. Reflecting on your creative experiences can deepen your understanding and amplify the benefits of your creative outlets.

Engaging in creative activities offers a powerful way to manage anxiety. Whether through art, music, writing, or crafting, these outlets provide emotional release, enhance self-awareness, and foster a sense of accomplishment and joy. By incorporating creative pursuits into your daily life, you can create a balanced and fulfilling approach to mental health and well-being.

COMBINING PHYSICAL AND MENTAL STRATEGIES

Combining physical and mental strategies offers a holistic approach to managing anxiety. This means integrating physical exercise with mindfulness practices and blending creative outlets with relaxation techniques. When you combine these elements, you create a comprehensive system that addresses both the body and mind, providing a more robust means of managing anxiety.

Imagine starting your day with a morning jog, followed by a few minutes of mindful breathing. Physical activity energizes your body and releases endorphins, while mindfulness helps you set a calm and focused tone for the day. This synergy can significantly enhance your emotional regulation, making it easier to navigate stressful situations with a clear and composed mind. Physical exercise, such as running or swimming, increases the production of neurotransmitters like serotonin and dopamine, which are essential for mood regulation. Complementing this with mindfulness practices, such as deep breathing or meditation, reinforces the benefits by helping you stay grounded and present.

Creating a balanced routine that incorporates both physical and mental strategies is crucial. Start by scheduling regular exercise sessions and mindfulness breaks throughout your week. For instance, you might commit to a 30-minute workout three times a week and a daily 10-minute mindfulness session. This consistency ensures that you're reaping the full benefits of both practices. Balance is vital, so make sure to allocate time for work, social activities, and self-care. If you have a demanding job, you might need to adjust your routine to fit in shorter, more frequent breaks rather than long, uninterrupted sessions.

Adjusting your routine based on your personal needs and preferences is essential for maintaining consistency and motivation. If you find that morning workouts don't fit well with your schedule, try evening sessions instead. Similarly, explore other forms like guided imagery or body scans if traditional meditation feels challenging. The goal is to create a sustainable and enjoyable routine rather than another source of stress.

The synergy of combining physical and mental strategies can significantly enhance their effectiveness. Improved emotional regulation is one of the main benefits. Physical activity helps to release the built-up tension and stress, while mindfulness practices allow you to process and manage your emotions more effectively. This combination can also enhance resilience, making it easier to bounce back from setbacks and maintain a positive outlook. When you integrate these strategies, you're more likely to stick with them, as the physical benefits motivate you to continue, and the mental clarity and calm reinforce the habit.

Consider the story of Laura, a professional who balanced yoga and journaling for mental clarity. She began with a yoga session each morning, focusing on breath and movement. Afterward, she spent a few minutes journaling her thoughts and intentions for the day. This routine helped her start her day with a clear mind and a sense of purpose, making it easier to handle work-related stress.

Then, there's Alex, a student who integrated nature walks with creative writing to relieve stress. He found that walking through a nearby park helped clear his mind and inspired his writing. By combining physical activity with a creative outlet, he managed his anxiety more effectively and found a productive way to express his thoughts and emotions.

Lastly, consider Erin, a parent juggling the demands of work and family life. She combined regular exercise with mindfulness to manage daily challenges. Each evening, after putting her kids to bed, she spent 20 minutes doing a home workout followed by a short mindfulness session. This routine helped her release the day's stress and provided a moment of calm before bed, improving her sleep quality and overall well-being.

By integrating physical and mental strategies, you create a robust system for managing anxiety. A balanced routine that includes regular exercise and mindfulness breaks can enhance emotional regulation, resilience, and motivation. Whether through yoga and journaling, nature walks and creative writing, or exercise and mindfulness, combining these strategies offers a comprehensive approach to mental health and well-being.

CHAPTER 10
COGNITIVE BEHAVIORAL TECHNIQUES

One afternoon, while sitting in a cozy corner of my favorite café, I overheard a conversation that reminded me of my own struggles with anxiety. A young woman was talking to her friend, expressing feelings of immense dread about a presentation at work. Her mind seemed to spiral into worst-case scenarios, much like mine used to. This got me thinking about cognitive distortions and how they contribute to our anxiety.

IDENTIFYING AND CHALLENGING COGNITIVE DISTORTIONS

Cognitive distortions are irrational, biased thoughts that warp our perception of reality. They act like funhouse mirrors, distorting our view of situations and often leading to heightened anxiety and stress. These distortions are automatic and habitual, making them difficult to recognize without conscious effort. They can take many forms, but their common thread is that they exaggerate the negative and minimize the positive, leading us to believe things are worse than they are.

One common cognitive distortion is catastrophizing. This involves always expecting the worst-case scenario. For example, if you make a minor mistake at work, you might think, "I'm going to get fired," even though there's no evidence to support this extreme outcome. Another frequent distortion is black-and-white thinking, where you view situations in all-or-nothing terms. If a project doesn't go perfectly, you might see it as a total failure, overlooking any positive aspects or learning opportunities.

Identifying your own cognitive distortions is the first step toward challenging and changing them. Keeping a thought diary can be immensely helpful in this process. Each time you feel anxious, write down the thoughts running through your mind. Over time, you will start to see patterns in your thinking. Recognizing these patterns is crucial because it allows you to pinpoint the specific distortions you tend to fall into. Additionally, using questionnaires or self-assessment tools designed to identify cognitive distortions can provide further insights into your thought processes.

Once you've identified your cognitive distortions, the next step is to challenge and reframe them. Start by asking evidence-based questions like, "What evidence supports this thought?" and "Is there any evidence that contradicts it?" This helps you to examine the validity of your anxious thoughts critically. For instance, if you find yourself thinking, "I'll never be able to handle this project," ask yourself, "Have I handled challenging projects before?" and "What skills do I have that can help me succeed?"

Considering alternative perspectives is another powerful technique. If you catch yourself in a negative thought spiral, try to view the situation from a different angle. Ask yourself, "How would a friend see this situation?" or "What would I say to someone else in this position?" This shift in perspective can reveal more balanced and realistic ways of thinking. Replacing negative thoughts with balanced, realistic ones is the ultimate goal. Instead of thinking, "I always mess things up," reframe it to, "I made a mistake, but I can learn from it and improve."

Practical exercises for cognitive restructuring can solidify these new ways of thinking. Thought records are a structured way to document and analyze your thoughts. Write down the situation, your automatic thoughts, the evidence for and against these thoughts, and then a more balanced thought. This practice helps reinforce the habit of questioning and reframing cognitive distortions.

Role-playing scenarios can also be beneficial. Practice responding to hypothetical situations with alternative perspectives. For example, if you're anxious about a job interview, role-play the interview with a friend, focusing on maintaining a balanced outlook. This can help you feel more prepared and less anxious when the actual situation arises.

Guided worksheets for cognitive restructuring provide a structured format for challenging and reframing thoughts. These worksheets typically include prompts and questions that guide you through the process of identifying, challenging, and replacing cognitive distortions. They can be instrumental when you're just starting out with cognitive-behavioral techniques.

Interactive Element: Thought Diary Template

Create a thought diary template to track your thoughts and identify cognitive distortions. Include sections for:

- the situation
- automatic thoughts
- emotions
- evidence for and against the thoughts
- more balanced thoughts

Use this template daily to practice cognitive restructuring and gain insights into your thought patterns.

Understanding and challenging cognitive distortions is a crucial step in managing anxiety. By recognizing these biased ways of thinking and using cognitive-behavioral techniques to challenge them, you can break the cycle of anxiety and develop a more balanced and positive mindset. This reduces anxiety and empowers you to face challenges with greater confidence and resilience.

DEVELOPING POSITIVE AFFIRMATIONS

Positive affirmations are potent tools for managing anxiety and improving self-esteem. They work by counteracting the negative self-talk that often fuels our anxious thoughts. Repeating positive affirmations creates new neural pathways in your brain, reinforcing positive thinking patterns. A shift in mindset can significantly impact your mental health. By focusing on positive statements, you train your brain to recognize and amplify your strengths, pushing aside the negative chatter that often dominates your thoughts.

Creating effective affirmations requires some thought and intention. The most impactful affirmations are those stated in the present tense and use positive language. Instead of saying, "I will not be anxious," you might say, "I am calm and in control." This phrasing reinforces the desired state rather than focusing on what you want to avoid. It's essential to focus on specific areas of improvement that resonate with your individual goals. For instance, if you struggle with self-worth, affirmations like "I am worthy of love and respect" can be incredibly empowering. Personalizing your affirmations ensures they resonate deeply with you, making them more effective.

Incorporating affirmations into your daily routine can make them a natural part of your thought process. One practical way to do this is by repeating your affirmations during your morning routine. As you brush your teeth or prepare breakfast, take a moment to say your affirmations out loud or in your mind. Writing them down in a journal can also reinforce their impact. The act of writing engages different parts of your brain, helping to solidify the positive statements. Affirmation apps or recordings can provide additional support, offering reminders and guided sessions to keep you on track.

Here are some specific examples of positive affirmations tailored to address various anxiety-related challenges:

- For general anxiety, you might say, "I am capable of handling whatever comes my way." This statement reinforces your ability to manage life's challenges.

- For issues related to self-worth, "I am worthy of love and respect" can help counteract feelings of inadequacy.
- If you struggle with staying present, try, "I choose to focus on the present moment." This affirmation can help ground you, reducing the likelihood of ruminating on past mistakes or future worries.
- For overcoming fears, "I have the strength to overcome my fears" serves as a powerful reminder of your inner resilience.

Reflection Section: Affirmation Journal

Start an affirmation journal to track the impact of your positive affirmations. Write down your chosen affirmations and reflect on how they make you feel. Note any changes in your mindset or anxiety levels over time. This practice can help you see the tangible benefits of positive affirmations and keep you motivated to continue using them.

By integrating these practices into your daily life, you can harness the power of positive affirmations to counteract negative self-talk and build a more positive, resilient mindset. These affirmations are not simply words; they are tools that can transform your relationship with anxiety, helping you to see yourself and your capabilities in a new, empowering light.

EXPOSURE THERAPY FOR ANXIETY

Exposure therapy is a powerful method for managing anxiety. It involves gradually exposing yourself to the situations or stimuli that trigger your fears. This controlled exposure helps reduce avoidance behaviors and build tolerance over time. The concept of habituation underpins this approach—by repeatedly facing your fears, the intensity of your anxiety diminishes, and you become more resilient. Imagine your anxiety as a fire alarm that goes off every time you make toast. Exposure therapy helps recalibrate that alarm so it only rings when there's an actual fire.

There are several types of exposure therapy, each tailored to different needs and situations. In vivo exposure involves facing real-life situations that trigger anxiety. For example, if you have a fear of public speaking, you might start by speaking in front of a small, supportive group before gradually moving to larger audiences. Imaginal exposure, on the other hand, involves visualizing feared scenarios. This can be particularly useful for situations that are difficult to recreate in real life, such as traumatic events. By vividly imagining these scenarios, you can process and reduce the anxiety they cause. Interoceptive exposure focuses on confronting the physical sensations of anxiety, such as a racing heart or shortness of breath. This type of exposure helps you become more comfortable with the bodily sensations that often accompany anxiety, reducing their power over you.

Implementing exposure therapy involves a structured, step-by-step approach. First, create a fear hierarchy by listing feared situations from least to most anxiety-provoking. This hierarchy acts as a roadmap, guiding you through the process of gradual exposure. Start with situations that cause mild anxiety and work up to more challenging scenarios. For instance, if you have social anxiety, your list might start with making small talk with a barista and progress to attending a large social gathering. Gradually facing these fears, starting from the bottom of the hierarchy, helps build confidence and reduce anxiety step by step.

During exposure sessions, it's crucial to use relaxation techniques to manage anxiety. Deep breathing, progressive muscle relaxation, and mindfulness can help keep you calm and focused. For example, before facing a feared situation, take a few minutes to practice deep breathing. Inhale slowly through your nose, hold for a couple of seconds, and exhale slowly through your mouth. This practice activates the parasympathetic nervous system, which counteracts the fight-or-flight response and helps you stay grounded.

Consider the case of Zoe, who struggled with social anxiety. By using exposure therapy, she gradually faced her fears of social interactions. She started with low-stakes situations, like making small talk with a cashier, and slowly worked her way up to attending social events. Over time, her anxiety diminished, and she became more comfortable in social settings.

Another success story involves John, who had a severe fear of flying. He began his exposure therapy by visiting an airport and familiarizing himself with the environment. Next, he watched flight videos and listened to airplane sound recordings. Eventually, John took short flights, gradually increasing the duration. Through these incremental steps, he significantly reduced his fear and could fly comfortably.

These examples highlight the transformative power of exposure therapy. By systematically facing your fears, you can reduce the hold anxiety has over you and build a more resilient mindset. The process is gradual and requires patience, but the rewards are well worth the effort. Exposure therapy offers a practical, effective way to confront and manage anxiety, helping you reclaim control over your life and face challenges with newfound confidence.

PRACTICAL APPLICATIONS OF CBT IN DAILY LIFE

Integrating CBT principles into your daily practice can provide a robust framework for managing anxiety. One of the most effective ways to apply these principles is through cognitive restructuring during stressful situations. When anxiety strikes, your thoughts can spiral out of control, making the situation seem far worse than it is. Cognitive restructuring helps you take a step back and evaluate these thoughts objectively. For instance, if you're anxious about an upcoming meeting, you might think, "I'm going to mess up, and everyone will judge me." Cognitive restructuring encourages you to ask, "Is there evidence to support this thought?" and "What's a more balanced perspective?" By challenging your initial thoughts, you can replace them with more realistic and calming alternatives.

Behavioral activation is another crucial CBT technique that is beneficial for combating avoidance. Avoidance can be a significant factor in maintaining anxiety. When you avoid a situation that makes you anxious, you reinforce the belief that the situation is dangerous, which only increases your anxiety over time. Behavioral activation pushes you to engage in activities even when you don't feel like it. For example, if you're avoiding social gatherings due to anxiety, start by attending a small, low-pressure event. Gradually increase your participation in social activities, and you'll find that your anxiety decreases as you build positive experiences.

Specific CBT techniques can be tailored to address common anxiety triggers. Performance anxiety at work is a frequent concern. To manage this, try breaking down tasks into smaller, more manageable steps. Practice relaxation techniques like deep breathing before presentations to calm your nerves. Visualization can also be helpful—imagine yourself performing successfully, focusing on the positive outcomes. For health anxiety, keep a symptom diary to track your concerns and see if they align with actual health issues. Challenge your anxious thoughts by asking, "What is the likelihood of this happening?" and "Have I felt this way before, and was it serious?" Social interactions can also be a significant source of anxiety. Use role-playing to practice conversations, focusing on staying present rather than anticipating what could go wrong.

Maintaining progress in CBT and preventing relapse requires ongoing effort. Regularly review and update your thought records to keep track of your cognitive restructuring progress. Set long-term goals to keep yourself motivated and focused. These goals can be anything from improving your public speaking skills to becoming more comfortable in social settings. Track your achievements to see how far you've come, which can be incredibly motivating. Seeking support from therapists or support groups can also provide additional encouragement and guidance. Regular check-ins with a mental health professional can help you stay on track and address any new challenges that arise.

Combining CBT with other anxiety management strategies can enhance its effectiveness. Integrating mindfulness practices with CBT techniques can help you stay grounded and aware of your thoughts, making it easier to catch and challenge distorted thinking. For instance, a short mindfulness session before engaging in cognitive restructuring can help you approach the process with a calm and focused mind. Physical exercise complements cognitive restructuring by reducing overall stress levels and improving mood. Regular physical activity can make it easier to maintain a positive outlook and build resilience. Dietary changes can also support behavioral activation.

Eating a balanced diet rich in nutrients can improve your overall well-being and energy levels, making it easier to engage in activities you might otherwise avoid.

Incorporating these practical applications of CBT into your daily life can provide a strong foundation for managing anxiety. By using cognitive restructuring and behavioral activation, addressing specific anxiety triggers, maintaining progress, and combining CBT with other strategies, you can build a more resilient and balanced life. Each small step contributes to your overall progress, creating a sustainable approach to mental well-being.

CHAPTER 11
LIFESTYLE CHANGES AND DAILY ROUTINES

One evening, as I was sorting through a chaotic pile of work emails, personal messages, and to-do lists, I realized that my life had become an overwhelming whirlwind of tasks and obligations. It felt like I was constantly juggling a dozen balls, always on the verge of dropping one. This constant state of stress was wearing me down, both mentally and physically. I knew something had to change, so I decided to take control by creating a balanced daily schedule. This simple yet powerful shift helped me find stability, focus, and a sense of calm amidst the chaos.

CREATING A BALANCED DAILY SCHEDULE

A balanced daily schedule is like a road map for your day, guiding you through tasks and responsibilities while ensuring you have time for self-care and relaxation. This structure is crucial for managing anxiety, as it helps reduce feelings of overwhelm by breaking down your day into manageable chunks. When you have a clear plan, it becomes easier to focus on one task at a time, increasing productivity and reducing stress. Additionally, a balanced schedule promotes a sense of control and stability, which is vital for maintaining mental well-being.

Identify your priorities and essential tasks to create a balanced schedule. Take some time to reflect on what truly matters to you and what needs to be accomplished each day. Make a list of these tasks, categorizing them by importance and urgency. This will help you see the bigger picture and prioritize your time effectively. Next, allocate specific time blocks for different activities. For example, set aside time in the morning for focused work, schedule a midday break for lunch and relaxation, and reserve the afternoon for meetings or collaborative tasks. Including buffer times for unexpected tasks or interruptions is also crucial. Life is unpredictable, and having some flexibility in your schedule can help you adapt without feeling overwhelmed.

Using tools and apps can make managing your schedule more manageable and efficient. Digital planners like Google Calendar or Trello allow you to organize your tasks and set reminders visually. Time management apps such as Todoist or TimeTree can help you track your progress and stay on top of deadlines. If you prefer a more tactile approach, physical planners and bullet journals can be great options. These tools help you plan your day and provide a sense of satisfaction as you check off completed tasks.

Adjusting and fine-tuning your schedule is an ongoing process. Regularly review and revise your schedule based on your needs and feedback. Set realistic goals and expectations for yourself, understanding that adjusting your plan as life evolves is okay. Balance is essential—ensure you allocate time for work, personal life, and self-care. Remember, a balanced schedule is not about cramming as much as possible into your day but creating a sustainable routine that supports your well-being.

A balanced daily schedule reduces overwhelm and stress by breaking down your day into manageable chunks. It ensures you have time for self-care and relaxation, which is crucial for maintaining mental health. By structuring your day, you increase productivity and focus, making it easier to tackle tasks efficiently. Moreover, a well-planned schedule promotes a sense of control and stability, providing a foundation for a more balanced and fulfilling life.

INCORPORATING SELF-CARE INTO YOUR ROUTINE

Understanding self-care is fundamental to managing anxiety and maintaining overall well-being. Self-care refers to activities and practices that promote physical, mental, and emotional health. It's about making a deliberate effort to take care of yourself, ensuring that you have the energy and resilience to meet life's demands. When you practice self-care, you actively work to prevent burnout and maintain your energy levels. This proactive approach enhances your quality of life and equips you with the tools needed to handle stress and anxiety more effectively.

There are various types of self-care, each catering to different aspects of well-being:

- Physical self-care involves activities that take care of your body, such as regular exercise, balanced nutrition, and adequate sleep. These activities are the foundation of good health and directly impact how you feel day-to-day.
- Emotional self-care focuses on activities that help you process and express your feelings. This can include journaling your thoughts, attending therapy sessions, or practicing mindfulness to stay grounded.
- Social self-care revolves around spending time with loved ones and setting boundaries to maintain healthy relationships. It's about finding balance in your social interactions, ensuring that you nurture connections that uplift and support you.
- Lastly, spiritual self-care involves practices that nourish your soul, such as meditation, nature walks, or engaging in religious activities. These practices help you find inner peace and a sense of purpose.

Creating a self-care plan to fit your needs is essential for making these practices a regular part of your life. Start by identifying your self-care needs and preferences. Reflect on what makes you feel energized, relaxed, and fulfilled. Everyone's self-care needs are different, so it's important to choose activities that ring true to you personally. Once you've identified these activities, set specific self-care goals. These goals should be realistic and doable, allowing you to gradually incorporate self-care into your routine without feeling overwhelmed. For example, if you enjoy reading, set a goal to read for 20 minutes each night before bed. If you find peace in nature, plan a weekly hike or visit to a local park. Scheduling regular self-care activities ensures that you prioritize these practices and make time for them amidst your busy schedule.

Incorporating self-care into your daily routine consistently can be challenging, but practical strategies can help. Use reminders and alarms to prompt self-care activities. Setting an alarm for a midday stretch or a reminder to meditate in the evening can ensure you don't overlook these important practices. Make self-care a non-negotiable part of your day. Treat it as an essential appointment with yourself that you can't cancel. Starting with small, manageable self-care practices can make the process less daunting. Begin with brief activities, such as a five-minute breathing exercise or a short walk, and gradually build up to longer sessions. The key is consistency and making self-care a habit.

Another effective strategy is integrating self-care into your existing routine. For instance, you can practice mindfulness while brushing your teeth or do a few stretches before you get out of bed in the morning. Combining self-care with daily activities makes it easier to stick to your plan. Additionally, finding a self-care buddy can provide motivation and accountability. Share your self-care goals with a friend or family member and check in with each other regularly. This support system can help you stay committed and celebrate your progress.

Self-care is not a luxury; it's a necessity. By understanding its importance and incorporating it into your daily routine, you can greatly improve your mental health and overall well-being. Whether it's through physical, emotional, social, or spiritual practices, self-care empowers you to take charge of your health and happiness.

THE ROLE OF HOBBIES AND PASSIONS

Engaging in hobbies and passions can be a powerful way to manage anxiety and enhance mental well-being. These activities provide a sense of joy and fulfillment that might be missing from the daily grind. When you immerse yourself in a hobby, you create a mental break from stress and worries, offering a healthy distraction that can rejuvenate your mind. This mental shift is crucial, as it allows you to step away from the constant demands of work and life, giving your brain a much-needed respite. Moreover, hobbies can enhance creativity and problem-solving skills, offering new perspectives and solutions to challenges you face. The act of creating or engaging deeply in an activity can also build confidence and self-esteem as you see tangible results from your efforts and realize your capabilities.

Identifying hobbies and passions that resonate with you is the first step. Reflect on past interests and activities that brought you joy. Think back to childhood or teenage years and remember what you loved doing before life became so busy. Sometimes, revisiting these old interests can reignite a passion you thought was long gone. If nothing comes to mind, consider exploring new hobbies through classes or workshops. Many communities offer a variety of classes, from pottery to dance to cooking. These environments provide a structured way to try new things and meet like-minded individuals. Additionally, trying different activities can help you find what resonates. Give yourself permission to experiment without the pressure of needing to excel immediately. The goal is to find something that you enjoy, and that provides a break from your routine.

Once you've identified hobbies that interest you, the next step is to incorporate them into your daily life. Setting aside dedicated time for hobbies is crucial. Block out specific times in your schedule, just as you would for work meetings or appointments. This dedicated time ensures that you prioritize your hobbies and make them a regular part of your routine. Creating a designated space for hobby activities can also help. Whether it's a corner of your living room for painting or a section of your kitchen for baking, having a specific area for your hobby makes it easier to engage without distractions. Balancing hobbies with other responsibilities can be challenging, but finding harmony is essential. Use your hobbies as a way to unwind after a busy day or as a break between tasks. This balance ensures that you don't neglect other responsibilities while still making time for activities that bring you joy.

- Gardening is a wonderful hobby for anxiety management. The connection with nature, the physical activity involved, and the satisfaction of seeing plants grow can be incredibly therapeutic. Tending to a garden allows you to be present at the moment, focusing on the task at hand and away from anxieties.
- Cooking or baking is another excellent hobby. It combines creativity with mindfulness, as the process of preparing food requires attention to detail and can be a sensory delight.
- Playing a musical instrument offers a form of emotional expression and focus. Whether you're strumming a guitar or playing the piano, music allows you to channel your emotions and immerse yourself in the melodies.
- Crafting, such as knitting, crocheting, or DIY projects, provides hands-on creativity and relaxation. The repetitive motions involved in these activities can be soothing, and the finished product gives a sense of accomplishment.

Engaging in hobbies and passions enriches your life and provides a valuable tool for managing anxiety. These activities offer a sense of fulfillment and joy, distract from stress, enhance creativity, and build confidence. By identifying what you love and making it a regular part of your routine, you create a balanced life that supports your mental well-being. Whether it's through gardening, cooking, playing music, or crafting, the key is to find something that resonates with you and brings you peace.

DEVELOPING A SUSTAINABLE EXERCISE ROUTINE

A sustainable exercise routine is a cornerstone for long-term anxiety management. Consistent physical activity not only boosts your physical health but also significantly improves your mental well-being. Regular exercise helps reduce stress and releases endorphins, the body's natural mood lifters. It enhances your overall mood, making you feel more positive and resilient. Additionally, staying active increases your energy levels, allowing you to tackle daily challenges with more vigor and less fatigue. When you commit to a regular exercise routine, you create a foundation for a healthier, more balanced life.

Creating a sustainable exercise routine begins with setting realistic and achievable fitness goals. It's important to start small and gradually increase the intensity and duration of your workouts. For instance, if you're new to exercise, begin with short, manageable sessions, such as a 10-minute walk each day. As you build your stamina, you can extend your workouts and include different types of exercises. Setting clear, attainable goals helps you stay motivated and track your progress. Remember, the key is consistency, not perfection.

Choosing enjoyable and varied exercises is crucial for maintaining a sustainable routine. When you engage in activities you love, exercise becomes something you look forward to rather than a chore. Explore different forms of physical activity to find what resonates with you. Whether it's dancing, swimming, hiking, or yoga, incorporating a mix of cardio, strength training, and flexibility exercises can keep your routine exciting and balanced. Variety prevents boredom and also ensures that you work different muscle groups, promoting overall fitness and reducing the risk of injury.

Scheduling regular workout sessions is another essential step. Treat your exercise time as a non-negotiable appointment with yourself. Block out specific times in your calendar for workouts, just as you would for important meetings or appointments. Having a set schedule helps you establish a routine and makes it easier to stick to your exercise plan. Additionally, consider your daily energy levels and choose times when you feel most motivated and energetic. Morning workouts provide a refreshing start to the day, while others prefer evening sessions to unwind after work.

Maintaining a consistent exercise routine can be difficult, especially when faced with common obstacles like lack of motivation or energy. On days when you feel unmotivated, remind yourself of the benefits of exercise and how it positively impacts your mood and well-being. Sometimes, just getting started is the hardest part. Commit to a short session, and often, you'll find the motivation to continue once you begin. Finding time for exercise in a busy schedule can also be difficult. Look for opportunities to incorporate physical activity into your daily routine. Take the stairs instead of the elevator, go for a walk on your lunch break, or do a quick workout while watching TV. Every little bit adds up and contributes to your overall fitness.

Addressing physical limitations or injuries is crucial to maintaining a sustainable exercise routine. Listen to your body and adjust your workouts as needed. If you have a specific injury or condition, consult with a healthcare professional or a certified trainer to develop a safe and effective exercise plan. Modify exercises to accommodate your limitations, and focus on activities that promote healing and prevent further injury. Remember, the goal is to stay active in a way that supports your health and well-being.

Practical tips can help you maintain a sustainable exercise routine. Mixing different types of exercise keeps your workouts exciting and balances the benefits of cardio, strength training, and flexibility. Using fitness apps or joining exercise classes can provide guidance and motivation. Many apps offer workout plans, track your progress, and even remind you to stay active. Group classes or online communities provide a sense of camaraderie and accountability. Track your progress and celebrate milestones to stay motivated. Keep a fitness journal or use an app to log your workouts and note improvements. Celebrate your achievements, no matter how small, to stay encouraged and committed to your fitness goals.

Incorporating these strategies into your exercise routine can make a big difference in managing anxiety and enhancing your overall well-being. A sustainable exercise routine supports both your physical and mental health, reducing stress, improving mood, and boosting energy levels. You can create a balanced and fulfilling fitness plan by setting realistic goals, choosing enjoyable activities, and addressing common challenges. As you continue this journey, remember that consistency and self-compassion are key. Celebrate your progress and stay committed to a healthier, happier you.

CHAPTER 12
PRACTICAL TOOLS AND RESOURCES

I remember the first time I walked into a support group meeting. My heart pounded, and my palms were sweaty. I felt a mix of fear and hope. But as I listened to others share their stories, I realized I wasn't alone. The room was filled with people who understood my struggles. That sense of community and belonging was a lifeline. It reminded me that seeking help and connecting with others could be transformative.

UTILIZING SUPPORT GROUPS AND THERAPY

Support groups can be a powerful resource in managing anxiety. They provide a sense of community and belonging, which is invaluable when you feel isolated by your struggles. Sharing experiences and coping strategies with others who understand your challenges can offer new perspectives and solutions. The emotional support and encouragement from group members can be incredibly uplifting, reducing feelings of loneliness and fostering a sense of connection. Hearing someone else voice an emotion or thought you've had can validate your own experiences and make you feel seen and understood.

Finding the right support group requires some research and trial and error. Start by looking into local and online support groups. Websites like the Anxiety and Depression Association of America (ADAA) offer directories of support groups. Consider the group size, format, and focus. Some groups may be large and structured, while others might be small and informal. Attend a few sessions to gauge your comfort and fit. It's essential to find a group where you feel safe and understood. Seeking recommendations from mental health professionals can also guide you toward reputable and effective groups.

Therapy is another cornerstone of anxiety management. Various therapeutic approaches can help you navigate your anxiety and build resilience:

- Cognitive behavioral therapy (CBT) is one of the most effective methods. It focuses on changing thought patterns that fuel anxiety. You can minimize their impact on your emotions and behaviors by identifying and challenging irrational thoughts.
- Dialectical behavior therapy (DBT) combines CBT with mindfulness practices. It emphasizes emotional regulation and distress tolerance, making it particularly useful for those who experience intense emotional reactions.
- Acceptance and commitment therapy (ACT) encourages you to accept your thoughts and feelings instead of fighting them. It focuses on committing to actions that align with your values, even in the presence of anxiety.
- Exposure therapy involves gradually facing your fears to reduce avoidance behaviors. By confronting anxiety-inducing situations in a controlled way, you build tolerance and reduce the power of those fears.

Starting therapy can feel intimidating, but it's a significant step toward managing anxiety. Begin by identifying your therapy goals and preferences. Do you want to focus on specific issues like social anxiety or general stress management? What type of therapist do you feel most comfortable with? Finding a qualified therapist can be done through directories like Psychology Today or referrals from your primary care doctor. Prepare for your first session by thinking about what you want to discuss and any specific concerns you have. Setting realistic expectations for therapeutic progress is crucial. Change takes time, and therapy is a process of gradual improvement.

Reflection Exercise: Therapy Goals Journal

Take a few moments to journal about your therapy goals. Write down what you hope to achieve in therapy, any specific issues you want to address, and what qualities you seek in a therapist. Reflect on how these goals align with your overall well-being and personal growth.

The combination of support groups and therapy provides a robust support system. While therapy offers personalized, professional guidance, support groups provide peer-based empathy and shared experiences. Both avenues can significantly enhance your ability to manage anxiety, offering tools and insights that you can apply in your daily life. Seeking help is not a sign of weakness but a sign of strength. These resources can empower you to take control of your mental health.

RESOURCES FOR FURTHER READING AND LEARNING

When anxiety feels overwhelming, the right book can offer much-needed insight and comfort. Over the years, I've turned to several books that have profoundly impacted my understanding of anxiety and provided practical strategies for managing it:

- *The Anxiety and Phobia Workbook* by Edmund J. Bourne is a comprehensive guide packed with exercises and techniques. It's like having a therapist in book form, offering step-by-step instructions to tackle anxiety head-on.
- Another transformative read is *Dare: The New Way to End Anxiety and Stop Panic Attacks* by Barry McDonagh. Barry's approach is unique and refreshing, focusing on embracing anxiety rather than avoiding it. His techniques help you confront and diminish panic attacks effectively.

- *The Anxiety Toolkit* by Alice Boyes is another gem. Alice breaks down complex concepts into simple, actionable steps that are easy to incorporate into daily life. Whether it's dealing with perfectionism or social anxiety, her book offers practical solutions.
- *When Panic Attacks* by David D. Burns uses cognitive behavioral therapy principles to help you understand and manage panic attacks. Burns' writing is engaging and empathetic, making it a must-read for anyone struggling with anxiety.

Books are just one way to deepen your understanding of anxiety. Online courses and workshops offer structured, in-depth learning experiences:

- Mindfulness-based stress reduction (MBSR) courses are particularly effective. These courses teach mindfulness meditation techniques that help reduce stress and improve emotional regulation.
- Online CBT courses from reputable institutions like the Beck Institute can equip you with tools to manage anxiety.
- Webinars and workshops on anxiety and mental health are also valuable. They provide expert insights and practical tips that you can apply immediately.
- Virtual retreats focused on relaxation and self-care offer an immersive experience, helping you unwind and rejuvenate without leaving your home.

Podcasts and videos are another excellent resource. They offer bite-sized, practical advice that you can listen to or watch on the go:

- "The Anxiety Coaches Podcast" features experts and real-life stories, providing a balanced mix of professional advice and relatable experiences.
- "The Calm Collective" focuses on mindfulness and meditation, offering tools to cultivate inner peace.

- "Anxiety Slayer" provides strategies and tips for managing anxiety, making it feel less overwhelming.
- YouTube channels like "The Anxiety Guy" and "Therapy in a Nutshell" offer valuable insights and practical tips.
- TED Talks on anxiety and mental health are also worth exploring. They feature experts sharing their experiences and research, providing new perspectives and solutions.

In today's digital age, various apps and tools can assist in managing anxiety:

- Meditation and mindfulness apps like Headspace, Calm, and Insight Timer offer guided sessions that fit into your busy schedule. These apps help you build a consistent mindfulness practice, providing a sanctuary of calm amidst the chaos.
- Mood-tracking apps like Daylio and Moodpath allow you to monitor your emotions and identify patterns. This self-awareness is crucial in managing anxiety.
- CBT-based apps like Woebot and Sanvello offer cognitive behavioral therapy techniques in a digital format. They guide you through exercises and provide support, making CBT accessible anytime, anywhere.
- Journaling apps like Journey and Reflectly help you reflect on your thoughts and feelings. They offer prompts and templates, making journaling a therapeutic practice that you can easily maintain.

Interactive Element: Anxiety Resource List

Create a personalized list of resources that resonate with you. Include books, courses, podcasts, apps, and any other tools that you find helpful. Refer to this list whenever you need guidance or support, and update it as you discover new resources.

Books, courses, podcasts, and apps each offer unique benefits, providing multiple avenues to explore and manage anxiety. By curating your own resource list, you create a personalized toolkit tailored to your needs. This empowers you to take control of your mental health, offering support and guidance whenever you need it.

CREATING YOUR PERSONALIZED ANXIETY MANAGEMENT PLAN

Crafting a personalized anxiety management plan starts with understanding your specific needs and goals. Each person's experience with anxiety is unique, so it's crucial to identify what triggers your anxiety and recognize any patterns. For example, you might notice that your anxiety peaks during social interactions or when you face tight deadlines at work. Reflecting on these patterns can provide valuable insights into areas that require more focus. Setting both long-term and short-term goals is essential. Short-term goals include practicing mindfulness daily or reducing caffeine intake, while long-term goals involve building resilience to stressful situations or improving sleep quality. Prioritizing areas for improvement, such as enhancing social interactions or establishing a consistent sleep routine, will help you create a targeted plan. Evaluate past strategies you've tried and consider their effectiveness. Did a particular breathing exercise help during a panic attack, or did journaling before bed improve your sleep? Use these reflections to inform your new plan, ensuring it builds on what has worked for you in the past.

An effective anxiety management plan includes several key components. Daily routines and habits are the foundation. Incorporating regular exercise, mindfulness practices, and balanced nutrition can significantly impact your mental health. Coping strategies for acute anxiety, such as deep breathing exercises, grounding techniques, and cognitive reframing tasks, provide immediate relief when anxiety strikes. Support systems offer ongoing guidance and encouragement, including therapy and support groups. Self-care and relaxation activities, like engaging in hobbies or creative outlets, help reduce stress and promote overall well-being. Integrating these elements into your plan creates a comprehensive approach to managing anxiety.

Creating a personalized plan involves gathering the necessary resources and tools. Start by collecting planners, apps, and journals that will help you track your progress. Setting SMART goals—Specific, Measurable, Achievable, Relevant, and Time-bound—ensures your objectives are clear and attainable. For instance, instead of setting an unclear goal like "reduce anxiety," specify that you want to "practice mindfulness for 10 minutes every morning for the next month." This helps you stay focused and motivated. Next, create a daily and weekly schedule for implementing your strategies. This schedule should include time for exercise, mindfulness practices, therapy sessions, and self-care activities. Regularly evaluate and adjust your plan based on your progress and feedback. If a strategy isn't working as well as expected, don't be afraid to tweak it. Flexibility is vital to maintaining an effective plan.

Let's look at some detailed examples of personalized anxiety management plans:

- For a working professional balancing work, family, and self-care, the plan might include morning mindfulness meditation, midday exercise, and evening family time. This individual could set short-term goals like practicing deep breathing during work breaks and long-term goals like improving work-life balance.
- Students managing academic stress and social anxiety might incorporate study schedules, regular exercise, and social exposure activities into their plans. Short-term goals involve attending a social event once a week, while long-term goals focus on building confidence in social settings.
- A retiree focusing on relaxation and community involvement could include daily walks, joining a local club, and engaging in creative hobbies. Their short-term goals involve participating in community events, and long-term goals could center on deepening social connections and enhancing overall well-being.

Creating a personalized anxiety management plan is a dynamic process that evolves with you. As you implement and refine your strategies, you'll better understand what works best for you. This plan serves as a road map, guiding you toward a more balanced and fulfilling life where anxiety no longer holds you back. By taking proactive steps and remaining flexible, you can effectively manage anxiety and enhance your overall well-being.

MAINTAINING PROGRESS AND PREVENTING RELAPSE

Consistency and commitment form the bedrock of any successful anxiety management plan. It's like building muscle; regular practice strengthens your resilience and reinforces positive habits and routines. This, in turn, prevents the re-emergence of anxiety symptoms and enhances your overall well-being. You create a stable foundation that supports mental health when you consistently engage in practices like mindfulness, exercise, and healthy eating. This stability is crucial because it helps you navigate life's ups and downs without being derailed by anxiety. Regularly practicing these habits makes them second nature, reducing the likelihood of slipping back into old, unhelpful patterns.

Tracking your progress and celebrating achievements is essential to maintaining your mental health. Using journals or apps to monitor your progress provides tangible evidence of your growth, helping you stay motivated. Set milestones for yourself and reward your accomplishments, no matter how small they may seem. Reflecting on positive changes and growth reinforces your efforts, making it easier to stay committed. Seek feedback from supportive friends or therapists to gain new perspectives and encouragement. Celebrating your achievements creates a positive feedback loop, which boosts your confidence and reinforces the belief that you can manage your anxiety.

It's important to stay vigilant about triggers and early warning signs to prevent relapse and maintain long-term progress. Regularly practice the anxiety management techniques you've learned, even when you feel good. This ongoing practice keeps your skills sharp and your resilience strong. Seek ongoing support from therapy or support groups to provide a safety net during challenging times. Adjust strategies as needed based on your changing circumstances. Life is dynamic, and your anxiety management plan should be flexible enough to adapt to new challenges and situations. By staying proactive and making adjustments, you can prevent minor setbacks from turning into major relapses.

When setbacks occur, seeking support is crucial. Don't hesitate to contact trusted family members or friends who can listen and offer emotional support. Schedule extra therapy sessions during high-stress periods to gain professional guidance and reassurance. Use crisis hotlines or online support communities if immediate help is needed. Practicing self-compassion is vital during these times. Avoid self-criticism and remind yourself that setbacks are a normal recovery process. Use these moments as opportunities to grow and learn rather than viewing them as failures.

Maintaining progress in anxiety management requires a balanced approach of consistency, self-awareness, and flexibility. By committing to regular practice, tracking your achievements, staying vigilant about triggers, and seeking support during setbacks, you can create a sustainable path to mental well-being. Remember, the goal is not perfection but progress. Each step you take, no matter how small, brings you closer to a more balanced and fulfilling life.

KEEPING THE CALM ALIVE

Now that you have everything you need to manage your anxiety, find balance, and boost your health, it's time to share what you've learned and help others on their journey.

By leaving your honest opinion of this book on Amazon, you'll show other readers struggling with anxiety where they can find the same help. Your review can guide them to the strategies that have made a difference for you and pass the knowledge forward.

Thank you for your support. Sharing our experiences keeps the journey to better mental health alive—and you're helping me do just that.

If you'd like to make a difference, scan the QR code below or follow the link to leave your review:

[https://www.amazon.com/review/review-your-purchases/?asin= B0DLKSPNNW]

REFERENCES

Acceptance and Commitment Therapy (ACT) – your nudge. (n.d.). https://your-nudge.com/acceptance-and-commitment-therapy-act/

Admin. (2023a, September 4). DOES YOGA HELP YOU LOSE WEIGHT - Beauty lies in healthy mind. Beauty Lies in Healthy Mind. https://healthybeautify.com/web-stories/does-yoga-help-you-lose-weight/

Admin. (2023b, October 15). The Importance of Self-Care for Mental Well-being - Ehime Love. ehime-love.com. https://ehime-love.com/the-importance-of-self-care-for-mental-well-being/

Admin, & Admin. (2023, December 4). 14 Natural anxiety Relief Remedies for Mental health. BearWalkingPal.com - Healthy Lifestyle Blog. https://bearwalkingpal.com/14-natural-anxiety-relief-remedies-for-mental-health/

Anthony, C. (2023, March 8). 30 positive affirmations for anxiety. Wealth Ideas Agency. https://www.wealth-ideas.com/30-positive-affirmations-for-anxiety/

Books of note. (1993). Journal of Traumatic Stress, 6(4), 593–594. https://doi.org/10.1007/bf00974329

Bourne, E. J. (2015). The Anxiety & Phobia Workbook. New Harbinger Publications.

Boyes, A., PhD. (2015). The anxiety toolkit: Strategies for Fine-Tuning Your Mind and Moving Past Your Stuck Points. Penguin.

Burns, D. D., MD. (2007). When panic attacks: The New, Drug-Free Anxiety Therapy That Can Change Your Life. Harmony.

Casey, P., & Bailey, S. (2011). Adjustment disorders: the state of the art. World Psychiatry, 10(1), 11–18. https://doi.org/10.1002/j.2051-5545.2011.tb00003.x

Devon. (2023, August 29). What Strategies Can Be Used to Incorporate Motivation into Daily Routines? - A.B. Motivation. A B Motivation. https://www.abmotivation.com/what-strategies-can-be-used-to-incorporate-motivation-into-daily-routines/

Elle, B., Elle, B., & Elle, B. (2024, March 26). 6 Surprising and Effective Techniques to Manage Stress You Haven't Tried Yet. Blogger Elle. https://www.bloggerelle.com/6-surprising-and-effective-techniques-to-manage-stress/?amp=1

Fitness, M. (2023, August 8). The power of mantra: managing stress and finding inner peace. Mantra Fitness. https://mantrafitness.com/the-power-of-mantra-managing-stress-and-finding-inner-peace/

4 tips for reducing or preventing anxiety. (n.d.). Texas Online Counseling. https://www.texonlinecounseling.com/blog/4-tips-for-reducing-or-preventing-anxiety

Griffiths, K. (2023, December 14). Self-Compassion. Path Of The Horse. https://www.pathofthehorse.com.au/post/self-compassion

How to identify and treat teen Depression. Parents. https://www.parents.com/teens/depression/teen-depression-statistics-causes-and-treatments/?utm_source=emailshare&utm_medium=social&utm_campaign=shareurl

Healthy habit stacking. (2023, December 12). The Esthetics Academy. https://estyacad emy.com/blogs/news/healthy-habit-stacking

Kendall, J. (2024, February 20). Forgotten Memories of Traumatic Events Get Some Backing from Brain-Imaging Studies. Scientific American. https://www.scientifi camerican.com/article/forgotten-memories-of-traumatic-events-get-some-backing-from-brain-imaging-studies/?fbclid=IwAR3IIWoeO3u1foawHOt4uKutATxEJH ba9lf6p-z2375vfrRJ6SaUfjv6HpY

McAdam, E. (n.d.). Therapy in a Nutshell. https://podcasts.apple.com/us/podcast/ther apy-in-a-nutshell/id1514880062

McDonagh, B. (2015). Dare: The New Way to End Anxiety and Stop Panic Attacks. Bmd Publishing.

Musetti, A., Cattivelli, R., Guerrini, A., Mirto, A. M., Riboni, F. V., Varallo, G., Casteln-uovo, G., & Molinari, E. (2018). Cognitive-Behavioral therapy: Current paths in the Management of Obesity. In InTech eBooks. https://doi.org/10.5772/intechopen. 72586

Payne, B. (2023, December 28). How did you make fitness a lifestyle Reddit | Personal Trainer Authority. Personal Trainer Authority. https://www.personaltrainerauthor ity.com/how-did-you-make-fitness-a-lifestyle-reddit/

Roychowdhury, D. (2024, March 8). Practicing Self-Care For Better Mental Health: A Comprehensive guide. Dr Dev Roychowdhury. https://www.drdevroy.com/self-care-mental-health-guide/

Ryan, G. (n.d.). The Anxiety Coaches Podcast. https://podcasts.apple.com/us/podcast/ the-anxiety-coaches-podcast/id908153168

Simsek, D. (n.d.). The Anxiety Guy. https://podcasts.apple.com/us/podcast/the-anxi ety-guy-podcast/id1080900600

Vander Leek, S., & Sivyer, A. (n.d.). Anxiety Slayer. https://podcasts.apple.com/us/ podcast/anxiety-slayer-with-shann-and-ananga/id348096293

Why practice mindfulness for resilience and coping skills? – recovery protocols. (2023, October 26). https://www.recoveryprotocols.com/why-practice-mindfulness-for-resilience-and-coping-skills/

Young, J. J. (2023, August 11). Navigating social anxiety. Quad Hautes Pyrenees - a New Way of Healing. https://www.quad-hautes